Sanitation for Primary Schools in Africa

Bob Reed and **Rod Shaw**

Illustrated by
Ken Chatterton

WEDC

WEDC

Water, Engineering and Development Centre
The John Pickford Building
Loughborough University
Leicestershire   LE11 3TU UK

Phone: +44 (0) 1509 222885   Fax: +44 (0) 1509 211079
Email: wedc@lboro.ac.uk   http://www.lboro.ac.uk/wedc/

Reed, R.A. and Shaw, R.J. (2008) *Sanitation for Primary Schools in Africa*
WEDC, Loughborough University, UK.

Technical illustrations by Ken Chatterton
Line illustrations by Rod Shaw

Peer reviewed by Sue Coates
Additional editorial contributions by Tricia Jackson

ISBN Paperback 978 1 84380 127 6

Developed from a strategic analysis of primary school infrastructure undertaken by
Bob Reed and Rose Lidonde for the WELL Resource Centre on behalf of DFID Kenya. Please note that views expressed in this book are not necessarily those of DFID.

Find out more about WEDC Publications online at:
http://www.lboro.ac.uk/wedc/publications/

Designed and produced at WEDC

This edition reprinted and distributed by Practical Action Publishing
Since 1974, Practical Action Publishing has published and disseminated books and information in support of international development work throughout the world. Practical Action Publishing trades only in support of its parent charity objectives and any profits are covenanted back to Practical Action (Charity Reg. No. 247257, Group VAT Registration No. 880 9924 76).

Contents

Introduction

Why sanitation is important

Health is the main reason given by governments, donors and non-governmental organizations for improving sanitation. The link between poor sanitation and poor health is very strong. Throughout the world, a child dies every eight seconds of a water-related disease and every year more than five million people die from a combination of dirty drinking water, dirty environments and the improper disposal of excreta. Millions more suffer nutritional, educational and economic loss through diarrhoeal disease that improvements in sanitation – especially human excreta management – can prevent. At the same time, human excreta are responsible for the transmission of a wide range of other diseases that infect millions of people.

Headteachers and school managers, who are especially concerned and responsible for the health of the school community, may also recognize that health is rarely the first answer that pupils or teachers give in response to questions about the benefits of improved sanitation facilities. Answers such as 'privacy', 'to reduce the smell', 'to make the school more attractive' or 'to get rid of flies and mosquitoes' may be far more common responses than 'improvements in health'.

All these reasons are valid and must be taken into account when planning sanitation improvements, as must the difference in objectives between those promoting sanitation improvements and those who will use the facilities throughout the course of the school day.

Investing in sanitation

It is usually easier to attract finance for improving water supply than for sanitation. However, investment in water supply alone will have a minimal impact on health without similar investments in sanitation and handwashing facilities. Collectively, a safe supply of water, clean sanitation facilities and the widespread practice of handwashing with soap will drastically reduce illness and death, particularly of children.

The primary health role of sanitation is to act as the first line of defence to disease transmission. As the diagram opposite shows, it prevents the organisms that transmit excreta-related diseases from escaping into the environment and infecting others. Locking excreta away in an enclosed receptacle such as a pit will also bring about immediate environmental benefits including a noticeable visual improvement, a reduction in foul odour and flies, and improvements to the quality of surface water resulting from a reduction of excreta polluting local water courses.

Sanitation and education

The primary role of schools, of course, is to help children learn. This is achieved not only through formal classroom education, but also by promoting good practice in daily living and setting an example. Habits and practices established at school can stay with pupils throughout their lives. When it comes to sanitation therefore, schools have a duty to promote good practice.

Establishing good sanitary practices in children – particularly the habit of handwashing with soap – not only helps them, but also helps the people around them. In many communities, the current generation is the first to receive formal education. The lessons they learn are taken home and passed on to their parents, brothers and sisters. This is an important route for transmitting information on basic family hygiene for the benefit of the whole community.

Sanitation and school management

Beyond the health and environmental benefits for children, teachers and the wider community, there are additional and equally persuasive reasons to invest in sanitation. The lack of adequate sanitation facilities is a major reason why many children, particularly girls, fail to attend school. The lack of facilities may well affect the performance and achievement of those who do attend, and is certainly detrimental to the working conditions of teachers. Sanitation, therefore, is not only important for health – it is central to the effective management of a school.

Note: In this book, the term 'sanitation' refers to the disposal of excreta (human faeces and urine) and small amounts of wastewater. It does not refer to the disposal of solid waste (garbage).

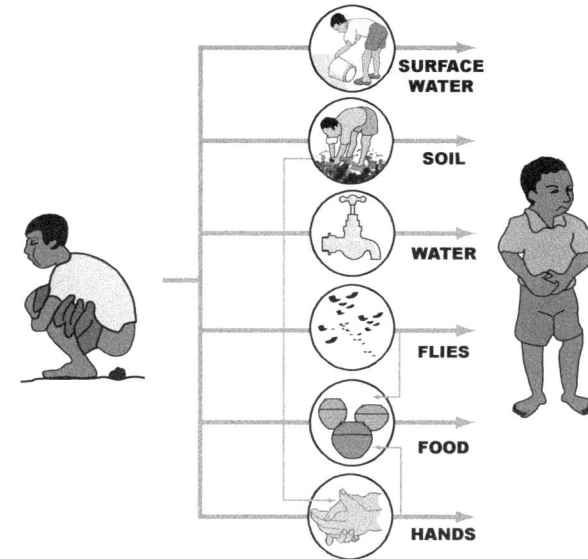

Common disease transmission routes from faeces

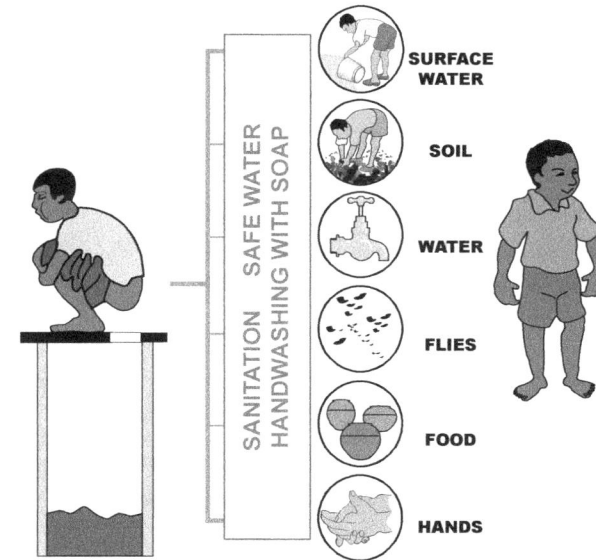

Sanitation, water and handwashing with soap act as a barrier to the spread of disease

3

About this book

Who this book is for

This book has been designed for a wide range of staff from agencies and government who have professional responsibilities for the provision of education and health throughout Africa. These include technical, design and architecture departments within ministries of education; district or local government education teams; district education officers and school inspectors working closely with school managers, headteachers and school communities; ministries of health; national and local water and sanitation agencies; and local and international non-governmental organizations specializing in water and sanitation.

How to use this book

The first step towards improving sanitation in schools is to assess the current situation and future needs so that appropriate decisions about improvements can be made. To do this and prioritize action, the tools for assessing sanitation, water supply and handwashing facilities can be used.

The guidelines can be used to help with the process of rehabilitating or decommissioning existing latrines, or for choosing the right type of latrine if new facilities are required.

Should this be necessary, all aspects of latrine design will need to be considered, including the construction method and materials to be used for the pits, the floors and the buildings themselves.

A number of illustrations of low-cost latrine blocks suitable for many rural and peri-urban locations are presented as a guide to selecting and specifying an appropriate design option.

There are also guidelines which help to decide where within the school compound the latrines should best be sited, and guidelines for developing a sustainable plan for the continuing operation and maintenance of the facilities.

The scope of this book

This book has been developed from a study of primary school infrastructure in Kenya, and although the recommendations presented here will be relevant to many other African countries, local customs and practice will need to be taken into consideration.

The book only considers pit latrines for sanitation as these are the cheapest, simplest and in many cases the most appropriate option for rural and peri-urban areas. Other specialist advice should be sought for alternative forms of sanitation such as pour-flush systems or sewerage. The book also limits the discussion of water to water supply at the point of use.

Refer to page 56 for other relevant sources of information.

Tools for assessing sanitation, water and handwashing in schools

Sanitation, water and handwashing

The health and well-being of pupils and staff in schools will be greatly enhanced if there are enough clean water and sanitation facilities and everyone adopts the practice of handwashing with soap. Some benefits will be gained from improving one or other of these but not as much as if all three are improved. So it is important that you carry out an assessment of all three – water, sanitation and handwashing with soap – to decide which needs to be improved the most.

These tools use simple assessment criteria that are divided into four categories and are assigned a score.

Are school facilities in need of improvement?

Scores

0 = The existing situation and facilities are acceptable. No improvement is necessary.

1 = The existing situation and facilities are reasonable but would benefit from improvement. Action is not necessarily a priority.

2 = The existing situation and facilities are very poor. Improvement is urgently required.

3 = There are no facilities. Provision is the highest priority.

Sanitation assessment

Assessment criteria

Assessment of sanitation facilities is based on three criteria: quantity, quality and usage. Only by considering all three will you be able to accurately assess the current situation.

Quantity refers to the number of facilities. For boys, this will include not only the number of cubicles, but also the length of the urinals. Quantity is easy to measure, so in many cases it is the only guide used for assessment. However, quantity alone does not present a true picture.

Quality refers to the condition of the facilities. A school may have many latrines but they will be unsafe to use if the floor is collapsing or the pit is full.

Usage refers to the suitability of the facilities for the people who use them. A school may have many latrines and they may be well constructed and in good condition but they will not be used if they are located in the wrong place or not designed to account for local customs and cultural sensitivities.

Start your assessment

- **Choose the relevant tools** from those provided opposite and overleaf (Tools 1, 2 or 3).

- **Compare the descriptions** given in the tables with the present situation. Refer to the detailed descriptions of quality and usage on page 10.

- **Assign scores** for each criterion to provide you with a general picture of the existing facilities. Assess girls' facilities separately from the boys' if you can.

- **Interpret your scores**. *The higher your score, the more urgent action becomes.* You will need to use your common sense to interpret your score. A score of 0 for quantity and 0 for quality, for example, may lead to the assumption that the situation overall is adequate whereas a score of 3 for usage would suggest that urgent action in that area is necessary.

- **Prioritize your actions** based on the results of your assessment.

If you are unsure about what to do, take a look first at the example given on page 9.

Tool 1: Assessment of sanitation facilities for children – *non-boarding*

Scores	0	1	2	3	Your scores
Quantity (users/cubicle)	Girls: 25 girls or less to 1 cubicle (minimum 4 cubicles) including 1 cubicle for disabled girls Boys: 50 boys or less to 1 cubicle (minimum 4 cubicles) including 1 cubicle for disabled boys *and* 50 boys or less to 1 metre of urinal	Girls: 26-35 girls to 1 cubicle (minimum 3 cubicles) Boys: 51-75 boys to 1 cubicle (minimum 3 cubicles) *and* 51-60 boys to 1 metre of urinal	Girls: 36 girls or more to 1 cubicle Boys: 76 boys or more to 1 cubicle *and* 61 boys or more to 1 metre of urinal	There are no latrines or urinals	
Quality	All structures are made to a high standard and there are no environmental hazards.	Most structures are made to a good standard but some major repairs are necessary.	Structures are in a poor condition, the pits are full and major reconstruction is required. Environmental hazards are likely.	There are no latrines or urinals	
Usage	The facilities provide for all the needs of girls and boys of different ages (including disabled children). There are no security or privacy risks. They are culturally acceptable and children use them.	The facilities provide for some of the needs of children of different ages and gender. There are potential security and privacy risks. Some children don't use them.	The facilities are poorly designed with little consideration of the needs of boys and girls of different ages. There are possible security risks and there is little or no privacy. They are culturally unacceptable so children won't use them.	There are no latrines or urinals	

Tool 2: Assessment of sanitation facilities for children – *boarding*

Scores	0	1	2	3	Your scores
Quantity (users/cubicle)	Girls: 7 girls or less to 1 cubicle (minimum 7 cubicles) including 1 cubicle for disabled girls Boys: 10 boys or less to 1 cubicle (minimum 5 cubicles) including 1 cubicle for disabled boys *and* 25 boys or less to 1 metre of urinal	Girls: 8-16 girls to 1 cubicle (minimum 3 cubicles) Boys: 11-30 boys to 1 cubicle (minimum 3 cubicles) *and* 26-35 boys to 1 metre of urinal	Girls: 17 girls or more to 1 cubicle Boys: 31 boys or more to 1 cubicle *and* 36 boys or more to 1 metre of urinal	There are no latrines or urinals	
Quality	All structures are made to a high standard and there are no environmental hazards.	Most structures are made to a good standard but some major repairs are necessary.	Structures are in a poor condition, the pits are full and major reconstruction is required. Environmental hazards are likely.	There are no latrines or urinals	
Usage	The facilities provide for all the needs of girls and boys of different ages (including disabled children). There are no security or privacy risks. They are culturally acceptable and children use them.	The facilities provide for some of the needs of children of different ages and gender. There are potential security and privacy risks. Some children don't use them.	The facilities are poorly designed with little consideration of the needs of boys and girls of different ages. There are possible security risks and there is little or no privacy. They are culturally unacceptable so children won't use them.	There are no latrines or urinals	

Tool 3: Assessment of sanitation facilities for staff

Scores	0	1	2	3	Your scores
Quantity (users/cubicle)	10 staff or less to 1 cubicle (minimum 2 cubicles – one each for men and women)	11-15 staff to 1 cubicle (minimum 2 cubicles – one each for men and women)	16 or more staff to 1 cubicle (1 cubicle for both men and women)	There are no latrines or urinals	
Quality	All structures are made to a high standard and there are no environmental hazards.	Most structures are made to a good standard but some major repairs are necessary.	Structures are in a poor condition, the pits are full and major reconstruction is required. Environmental hazards are likely.	There are no latrines or urinals	
Usage	The facilities provide for all the needs of staff (including disabled members of staff). There are no security or privacy risks. They are culturally acceptable and staff use them.	The facilities provide for some of the needs of staff. There are potential security and privacy risks. Some staff don't use them.	The facilities are poorly designed with little consideration of the needs of staff. There are possible security risks and there is little or no privacy. They are culturally unacceptable so staff won't use them.	There are no latrines or urinals	

Example

A school has 500 girl pupils and 25 latrine cubicles but they are in poor condition with the cubicle doors missing and the walls falling down. The latrine drop holes are large and small children are frightened to use them.

A zero score is marked against quantity as the number of cubicles is adequate (500 ÷ 25 = 20 children per cubicle). However, such a school would score perhaps 2 for quality and 1 for usage.

This demonstrates that the school does not need to construct any more latrines but it does need to renovate the ones it has and adapt some of them to suit the needs of small children.

Definitions of latrine quality and usage

Quality

A good quality latrine has a solid superstructure (the part of the building above ground) with doors to each cubicle and a roof. The cubicles are large enough for children to enter and squat comfortably. There is sufficient light to enable children to use the latrine correctly and feel safe. The floor is made of concrete or similar durable material, is smooth and free draining.

Where a pit is used, the pit walls are lined – at least for the top metre – and access is provided for emptying. For other disposal options, adequate provision is made for maintenance and the disposal of waste liquids.

There should also be facilities for handwashing with soap and, if appropriate, for girls to bathe or change during their periods of menstruation. Facilities for disabled people are appropriate for their needs and easily accessible from the rest of the school. There is no risk of pollution from the latrines, particularly to local water sources.

Urinals are made of durable materials that are easy to clean and are free draining. Proper arrangements are made for the disposal of urine. (A roof for urinals is not essential except in areas where it often rains.) See pages 23-41 for designs that meet these criteria.

Usage

Latrines should be located and arranged so that pupils and staff are happy to use them in the correct way. This includes considerations of security and privacy from each other, from the opposite sex and from outsiders. The latrine cubicles should be designed to suit the gender and the age group of the users.

Handwashing facilities and soap should be placed in a suitable location and at an appropriate height.

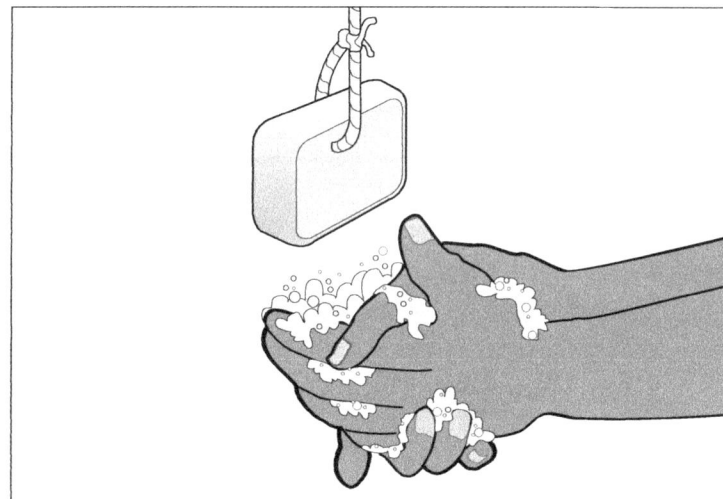

Water supply assessment

Assessment criteria

As with the assessment of sanitation facilities, assessment of a school's water supply is also based on three criteria, this time: quantity, quality and convenience. Again, only by considering all three will you be able to assess the current situation accurately.

Quantity refers to the amount of water provided per child per day. Generally, this will also include the provision of enough water for staff but not for high water use activities such as irrigation or washing large floor areas.

Quality relates to how clean and safe the water is. It is strongly recommended that the water supply is professionally tested for quality. If this is not possible, the descriptions given in the tables will give you a general indication.

Convenience relates to how easy it is for children and staff to reach the water point and use it in the correct way. This includes the distance to the water source and the design of the water collection point.

Start your assessment

- **Choose the relevant tools** from those provided overleaf (Tools 4, 5 or 6).

- **Compare the descriptions** given in the tables with the present situation.

- **Assign scores** for each criterion to provide you with a general picture of the existing facilities.

- **Interpret your scores**. *The higher your score, the more urgent action becomes.* You will need to use your common sense to interpret your score. A score of 0 for quantity and 0 for quality, for example, may lead to the assumption that the situation overall is adequate whereas a score of 3 for convenience would suggest that urgent action in that area is necessary.

- **Prioritize your actions** based on the results of your assessment.

If you are unsure about what to do, take a look first at the example given on page 13.

11

Tool 4: Assessment of water supply where pit latrines are used

Scores	0	1	2	3	Your scores
Quantity Day schools Boarding schools	15 litres per child per day 30 litres per child per day	10 litres per child per day 20 litres per child per day	5 litres per child per day 10 litres per child per day	There is no water supply	
Quality	Acceptable colour and taste. There is no evidence that it causes sickness.	Sometimes the water has poor colour or taste or causes sickness.	The water has poor colour or taste or causes sickness if not boiled before use.	There is no water supply	
Convenience	There are multiple water points around the school compound which are well designed and constructed.	There is a single water point in school and it is well designed and constructed.	The water point is more than 500m from school, is poorly constructed and has not been designed with children in mind.	There is no water supply	

Tool 5: Assessment of water supply where flush latrines are used

Scores	0	1	2	3	Your scores
Quantity	120 litres per child per day	100 litres per child per day	75 litres per child per day	There is no water supply	
Quality	Acceptable colour and taste. There is no evidence that it causes sickness.	Sometimes the water has poor colour or taste or causes sickness.	The water has poor colour or taste or causes sickness if not boiled before use.	There is no water supply	
Convenience	There are multiple water points around the school compound which are well designed and constructed.	There is a single water point in school and it is well designed and constructed.	The water point is more than 500m from school, is poorly constructed and has not been designed with children in mind.	There is no water supply	

Tool 6: Assessment of handwashing facilities

Scores	0	1	2	3	Your scores
Quantity of handwashing facilities in school	1 washing point per 50 pupils	1 washing point per 100 pupils	1 washing point per 200 pupils	No washing points	
Quality of facilities with water and soap for handwashing	All water points are provided with soap	60% of water points are provided with soap	40% of water points are provided with soap	No water or soap provided	
Convenience of handwashing facility	Conveniently placed handwashing facilities within 10 metres of all latrines, cooking and eating areas	Conveniently placed handwashing facilities close to 50% of latrines, cooking and eating areas	Some handwashing facilities available but not close to latrines or cooking and eating areas	No convenient facilities	

Example

A school obtains its water supply from a shallow well dug in the centre of the school compound. There is enough water for the school's needs all year round. The water is generally of good quality except after heavy rains when it turns muddy. When it is muddy, it is also noticed that many of the children suffer with diarrhoea. The school has pit latrines.

Such a school would score 0 or 1 for quantity because there is plenty of water for the school even though the quantity has not been measured. It would score 1 for quality and 1 for convenience.

This would indicate that the school's water supply is satisfactory but could be improved. A discussion with the school's technical adviser would lead to the suggestion that the area around the top of the well should be improved, as well as the method used for abstracting the water.

Handwashing assessment

Assessment criteria

An assessment of children's knowledge and practice of handwashing with soap is an indicator of the overall standard of hygiene in the school, but it may not reflect the overall standard of health as problems may be caused by inadequate sanitation facilities or a lack of a safe water supply. The results of an assessment of handwashing therefore, will normally need to be considered alongside the sanitation and water supply assessments. For example, a situation where the average incidence of disease is high, but the scores for the handwashing criteria are low, may suggest that the sanitation and/or the water supply facilities need to be improved.

Start your assessment

- **Compare the descriptions** given in Tool 7 opposite with the present situation.

- **Assign scores** for each criterion to provide you with a general picture of the level of understanding of the importance of handwashing with soap in relation to sanitation as well as the level of practice itself. *Remember, the higher your score for each criterion, the more urgent action becomes.*

- **Prioritize your actions** based on the results of this assessment and your sanitation and water supply assessments.

Example

A school of 1000 children has an average of 3 incidences of diarrhoea per pupil per year. A survey of the curriculum shows that hygiene education is well covered within the syllabus. Interviews with children showed that 75% knew the signs and symptoms of diarrhoea and how it could be prevented. However, it was also noticed that less than 20% of children washed their hands with soap after visiting the latrine or before eating food.

This would indicate that either:

- the children were not putting their knowledge into practice and more effort was needed to help them adopt the practice of handwashing with soap in the school; or

- there are insufficient water supply and/or sanitation facilities in the school; or

- the children's home environment is uniformly poor and all are being infected out of school hours; or

- the water supply is polluted.

The assessment has shown you that there is a problem but more work needs to be done to find out what the true cause is.

Tool 7: Assessment of the practice of handwashing with soap

Scores	0	1	2	3	Your scores
Average incidence of any of the diseases listed below per child per year *.	Less than 1	1 – 2	2 – 4	More than 4	
Percentage of pupils able to describe signs and symptoms of the disease	More than 80%	50-80%	20-50%	Less than 20%	
Percentage of pupils able to describe how diseases are related to water and sanitation (appropriate to the child's age).	More than 80%	50-80%	20-50%	Less than 20%	
Percentage of pupils able to describe appropriate measures to prevent infection (appropriate to the child's age).	More than 80%	50-80%	20-50%	Less than 20%	
Percentage of pupils washing hands thoroughly with soap after using the latrine**	More than 80%	50-80%	20-50%	Less than 20%	
Percentage of pupils washing hands thoroughly with soap before touching, preparing or eating food**	More than 80%	50-80%	20-50%	Less than 20%	

Notes: * Diseases include: diarrhoea, worm infection and skin infection. You need only consider those present in the area.   ** Refer to page 55: 'How to wash hands thoroughly'.

Guidelines for rehabilitating and decommissioning existing latrines

Rehabilitation

Many schools have latrine blocks that are not being used. It may be more appropriate to rehabilitate these than construct new ones. If rehabilitation is not possible then the block should be removed (decommissioned) for safety and environmental reasons. This section describes how an existing latrine could be rehabilitated or decommissioned, looking at the most common problems and ways of overcoming them.

What to do when the pit is full

All pit latrines will eventually fill and a decision then has to be made whether to empty the pits or abandon them and build new latrines. In most cases it is sensible to empty school latrines because the cost of emptying is much less than the cost of constructing new ones.

The first consideration is how to gain access to the pit contents. There is no problem with latrines fitted with an access hatch to the pit, but many do not have them. In such cases, the best approach is to demolish one of the latrine cubicles and break open the floor slab. When emptying is complete, a plain concrete slab can be made to cover the hole so that next time emptying is much easier.

Manual emptying is not recommended because it exposes workers to contamination and is usually messy and odorous. Often, however, there is no alternative and so all necessary steps should be taken to make the process as safe and hygienic as possible.

Arrange to empty the pit just before the end of the main school holiday. The contents will then have had time to decompose and dry out. If possible, employ a professional emptying team. They will have all the necessary equipment and carry out the emptying in the shortest time. In any case, make sure that all workers are provided with full protective clothing and there are facilities for them to wash after finishing work.

Make sure there is more than one opening into the pit and, if possible, set up a fan (or light a fire) near to one of the openings to create a flow of air through the pit. This will reduce odour problems for the workers and minimize the risk of a build up of harmful gas. If the contents are dry, they can be dug out using a spade and bucket.

The best way to empty a pit is to use a vacuum tanker. These are commonly found in urban areas and one might be available near to you. The vacuum tanker can only suck up liquids so the pit contents will have to be mixed with water first. Most vacuum tankers, however, will not be able to suck up the pit contents if the children have used solid objects such as stones, corn cobs or sticks for anal cleansing as they will block the suction pipe.

In rural areas, the easiest way of disposing of the sludge is to dig a hole and bury it. The sludge should not be spread on the surface or used as a fertilizer as it will contain harmful organisms that could spread disease.

What to do if the pit lining has collapsed

Damaged pit linings can sometimes be repaired but the operation can be very dangerous. Not only could the walls or floor slab fall on the workers carrying out the repairs but the workers could be overcome by poisonous gas from the pit sludge. Small damaged areas could be repaired, but it is essential that the pit is emptied first and is well ventilated during the repair process. It is important to provide the workers with safety harnesses so that they can be lifted from the pit in an emergency.

A common cause of a collapsed lining is the lack of drainage holes in the wall. Surface water collects between the wall and the surrounding ground and this creates high pressure that causes the wall to collapse. Making sure all the walls have holes in them prevents the likelihood of this happening.

What to do if the floor slab is damaged

If the floor slab has started to collapse, this indicates that there is either a non-existent or damaged pit lining (see above) or that the original slab was poorly constructed. In either case, the latrine cubicles will have to be removed. If the pit has no lining at all, the slab will have to be completely removed and a pit lining constructed, at least to a depth of one metre. It may then be possible to place the old floor slab on the new lining, but most likely a new slab will be required.

If the problem lies with the existing floor slab, then it will have to be removed and a new one constructed to replace it. In both cases the latrine cubicles will have to be demolished and rebuilt.

What to do if the latrine block is damaged

Most latrine blocks become damaged over time due to vandalism and general wear and tear. In the long run, it is better to repair buildings on a regular basis than wait until major damage has been caused. In all cases, use the best available materials and heavy-duty designs, as these will last longer and save money over time.

Improving access and privacy

Another common problem with latrine blocks is access. Many have floor slabs above ground level, which makes access difficult, particularly for disabled children. Use compacted soil or concrete to raise the floor level around the latrine to the same level as the pit floor.

Privacy will be greatly improved by the installation of a privacy wall in front of the latrine doors.

Remember to install handwashing facilities close to the latrine block.

Decommissioning

If the existing latrine block is not worth repairing it should be decommissioned. Leaving the latrine in place will be unsightly, dangerous and will attract vandals and vermin.

Demolish the latrine cubicles – it may be possible to re-use the materials for another building. Dig up the floor slab, break it into small pieces and dispose of them to a managed waste tip – or bury them. Remove as much of the pit lining as possible. This too may be re-used on another building. Level the contents of the pit and cover them to ground level or slightly above with soil. Plant trees or bushes on top of the pit. They will grow well on the nutrients from the pit sludge.

Demolishing a latrine block can be a dangerous activity. Make sure all workers wear protective clothing such as safety boots and hats, and that there is an agreed plan for helping someone who has fallen into the pit.

Trees and bushes grow well on nutrients from the pit sludge

Guidelines for choosing the right type of latrine for a school

Appropriate design

This book focuses on the pit latrine because it is the most appropriate technology (and the cheapest) for many situations. If pit latrines are not appropriate, or you prefer to look at other options, you should seek specialist advice.

If you decide to go ahead and build pit latrines you will have to select the most appropriate design. In most cases, one of the designs shown on the accompanying drawings should be suitable but latrine selection can be a complex process and so you are still encouraged to seek local specialist advice and support.

There are two stages in the process of selection. The first is to select the most suitable type of pit latrine and the second is to decide what materials to use.

Selecting the right type of pit latrine

Follow the flow chart shown over the page to choose the most appropriate type of pit. It may be that more than one arrangement is possible.

Selecting construction materials

Latrines can be built using a wide range of materials but it is important to choose materials that suit local conditions. The pit lining will normally be made of either burnt bricks, cement blocks or local stone.

It is strongly recommended that the floor of the latrine is made of reinforced concrete. Other materials such as wood can be used but they are more difficult to keep clean and will eventually become dangerous as the wood rots or is eaten by insects. Simple squatting holes are pictured in the illustrations, but you can also install pedestal toilets over the holes. These will be more expensive however.

The latrine building and roof can be made of a wide variety of materials, some of which are illustrated in the accompanying drawings. The choice should be based on cost, the availability of the raw materials, ease of construction by local builders, ease of maintenance and the style of architecture of other buildings in the local area.

Where to go for specialist advice

A number of organizations may be able to offer specialist advice:

* Technical or architect departments of the Ministry of Education

* National or local water and sanitation departments

* The Ministry of Health

* Non-governmental organizations specializing in water and sanitation such as Oxfam, WaterAid etc.

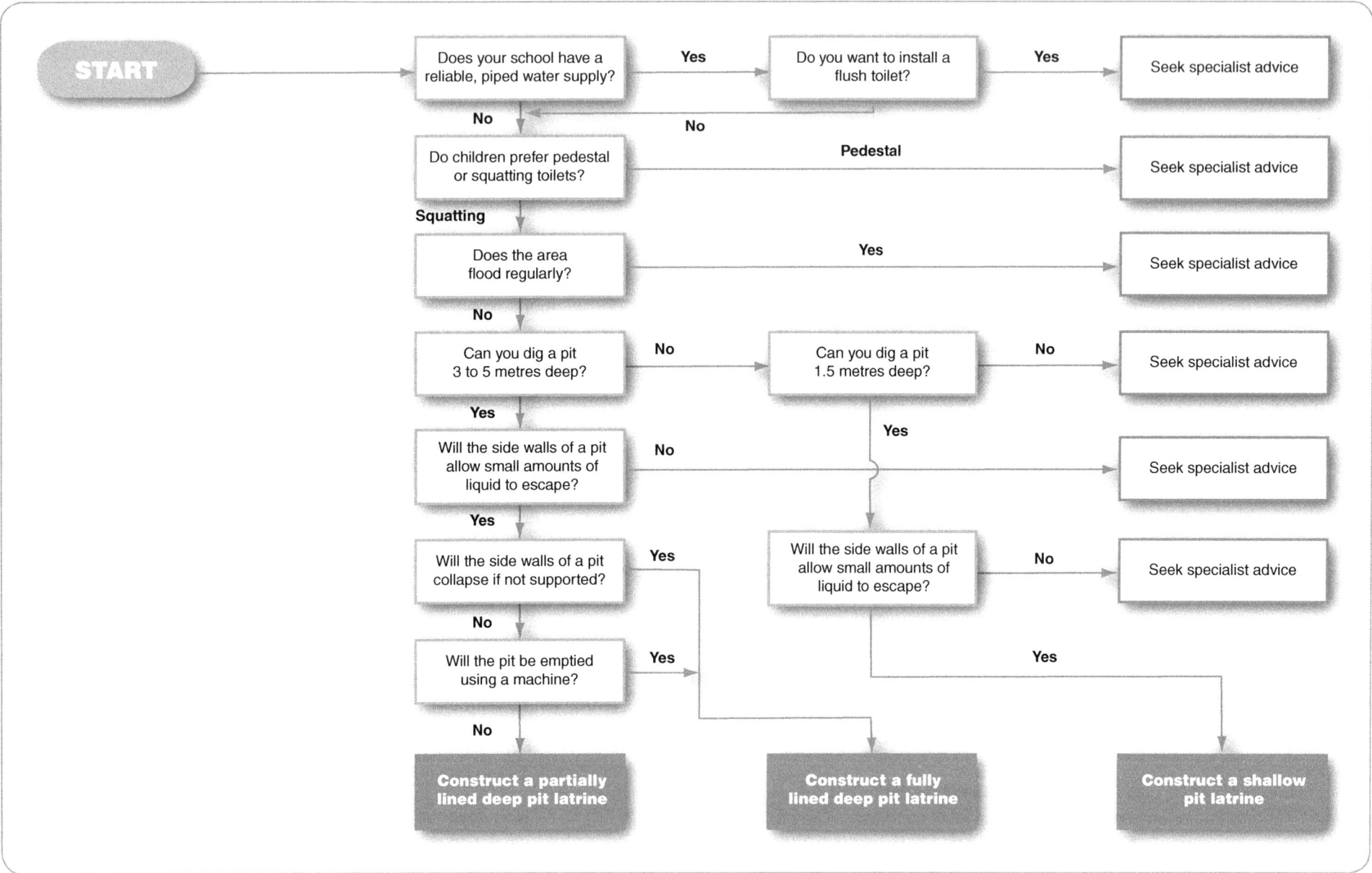

A guide to selecting the right type of latrine for a school

START

Does your school have a reliable, piped water supply? — **Yes** → Do you want to install a flush toilet? — **Yes** → Seek specialist advice

Do you want to install a flush toilet? — **No** ↑

Does your school have a reliable, piped water supply? — **No** ↓

Do children prefer pedestal or squatting toilets? — **Pedestal** → Seek specialist advice

Squatting ↓

Does the area flood regularly? — **Yes** → Seek specialist advice

No ↓

Can you dig a pit 3 to 5 metres deep? — **No** → Can you dig a pit 1.5 metres deep? — **No** → Seek specialist advice

Yes ↓ (3 to 5 metres)

Will the side walls of a pit allow small amounts of liquid to escape? — **No** → Seek specialist advice

Yes (1.5 metres, Can you dig a pit 1.5 metres deep?)

Yes ↓

Will the side walls of a pit collapse if not supported? — **Yes** →

Will the side walls of a pit allow small amounts of liquid to escape? — **No** → Seek specialist advice

No ↓

Will the pit be emptied using a machine? — **Yes** →

No ↓

Construct a partially lined deep pit latrine

Construct a fully lined deep pit latrine (Yes)

Construct a shallow pit latrine (Yes)

Illustrations of school latrines

What these illustrations are for

The illustrations in this section of the book present a range of options for building new sanitary facilities. They show latrines constructed of various materials and for different ground conditions.

The illustrations are not engineering drawings and should not be used for detailed design of the buildings. They can, however, be used to form the basis of a detailed design specification. They have been produced as three-dimensional projections for ease of understanding.

Primarily aimed at rural schools, these designs are also appropriate for schools in peri-urban areas where latrines do not have to be built next to other buildings, and where water use is limited. Schools connected to a municipal sewerage system may need to consider alternative designs.

How to use the illustrations

The illustrations are presented in sets to show the designs as they would appear during the process of construction. The first set shows construction below the ground, the second set shows the construction of the floors, and the third set shows the design of the buildings (or 'superstructures'). Following these sets are further illustrations of alternative roof and door materials, low-cost handwashing facilities and designs for simple water points.

'Pick and mix'

Most of the components of the latrines are designed to be interchangeable. To choose the most appropriate design for a school, start by deciding what type of ground conditions there are and what building materials you would prefer to use. Then select the most appropriate design for the below ground component, followed by the ground level component and finally the above ground component. You do not have to use the same materials for the superstructure as you use below ground.

The designs for situations where only a shallow pit can be dug are different. They are based on using two pits alternately. The pits from one set (usually known as 'twin pits') are filled and then sealed while pits from the second set are used. When the pits from the second set are filled, the first set of pits can be emptied and re-used (see page 51).

Most of the illustrations are of latrine blocks for boys to show the design of the urinals too, but there are also design layouts for girls' latrines. Any of the materials used for the boys latrines can also be used for the girls.

The illustrations

Set 1: Below ground construction

These illustrations show the components of the latrine below ground level. All designs are based on the pit latrine as this is usually the cheapest and most appropriate design to use for rural schools. Designs are shown for different building materials and different ground conditions.

Set 2: Floor construction

These illustrations show the ground level components of the latrine blocks. All of these use a floor slab made of reinforced concrete.

Set 3: Above ground construction ('superstructures')

These illustrations provide ideas for building in a variety of materials such as burnt brick and mud. All follow the same basic layout with a block containing four cubicles and a urinal for boys and four cubicles and a changing and bathing room for girls to use during menstruation.

Set 4: Alternative roof and door materials

Additional detailed illustrations of alternative roof and door components and materials

Set 5: Handwashing and water points

Low-cost handwashing devices and water point designs

Guidelines

Figure 1.1. Cement block or burnt brick, fully lined (boys)

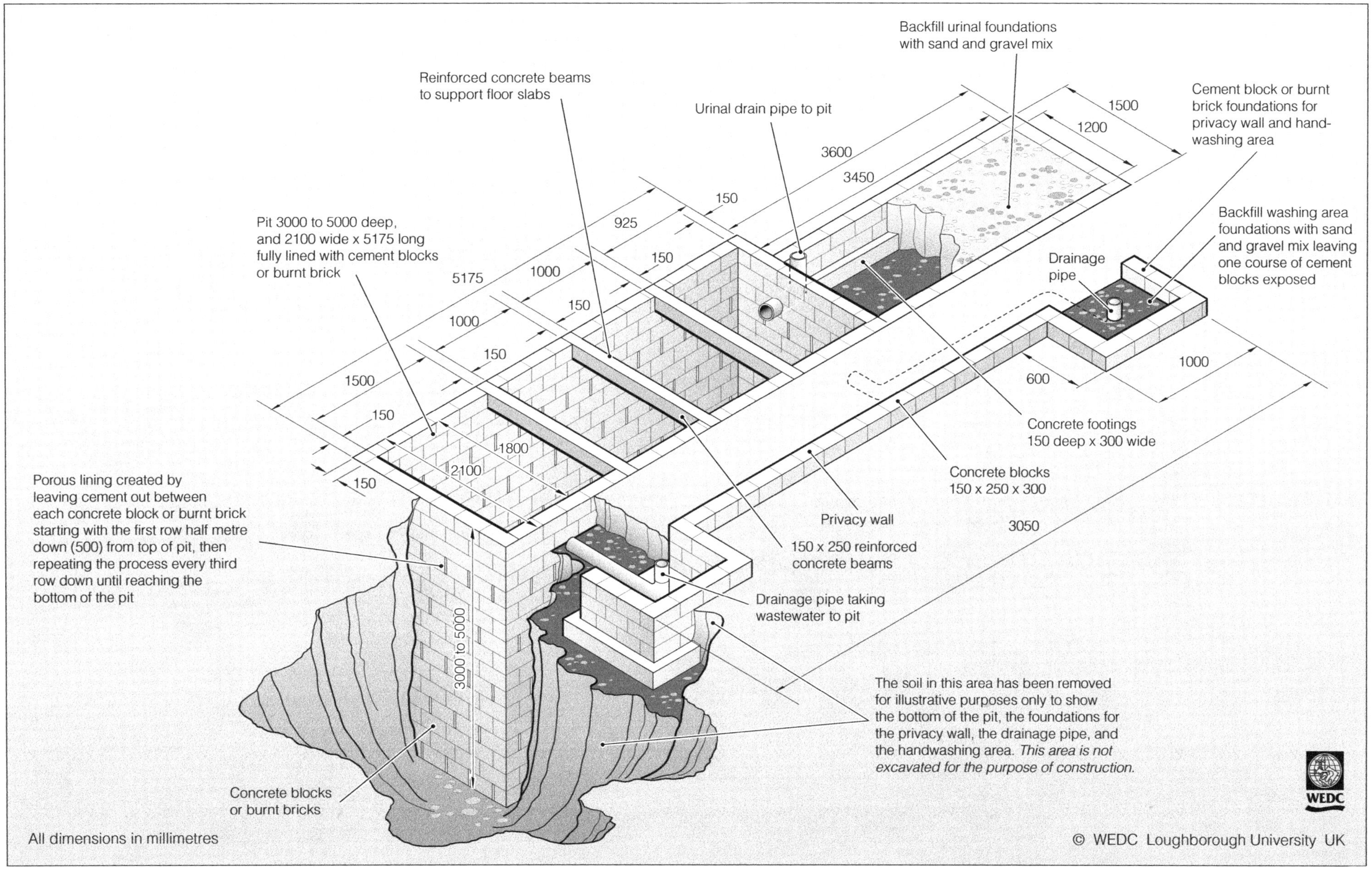

Backfill urinal foundations with sand and gravel mix

Reinforced concrete beams to support floor slabs

Urinal drain pipe to pit

Cement block or burnt brick foundations for privacy wall and hand-washing area

Pit 3000 to 5000 deep, and 2100 wide x 5175 long fully lined with cement blocks or burnt brick

Backfill washing area foundations with sand and gravel mix leaving one course of cement blocks exposed

Drainage pipe

Porous lining created by leaving cement out between each concrete block or burnt brick starting with the first row half metre down (500) from top of pit, then repeating the process every third row down until reaching the bottom of the pit

Concrete footings 150 deep x 300 wide

Concrete blocks 150 x 250 x 300

Privacy wall

150 x 250 reinforced concrete beams

Drainage pipe taking wastewater to pit

The soil in this area has been removed for illustrative purposes only to show the bottom of the pit, the foundations for the privacy wall, the drainage pipe, and the handwashing area. *This area is not excavated for the purpose of construction.*

Concrete blocks or burnt bricks

1500
1200
3600
3450
150
925
150
5175
1000
1000
150
1500
150
150
1800
2100
150
3000 to 5000
600
1000
3050

All dimensions in millimetres

WEDC

Guidelines

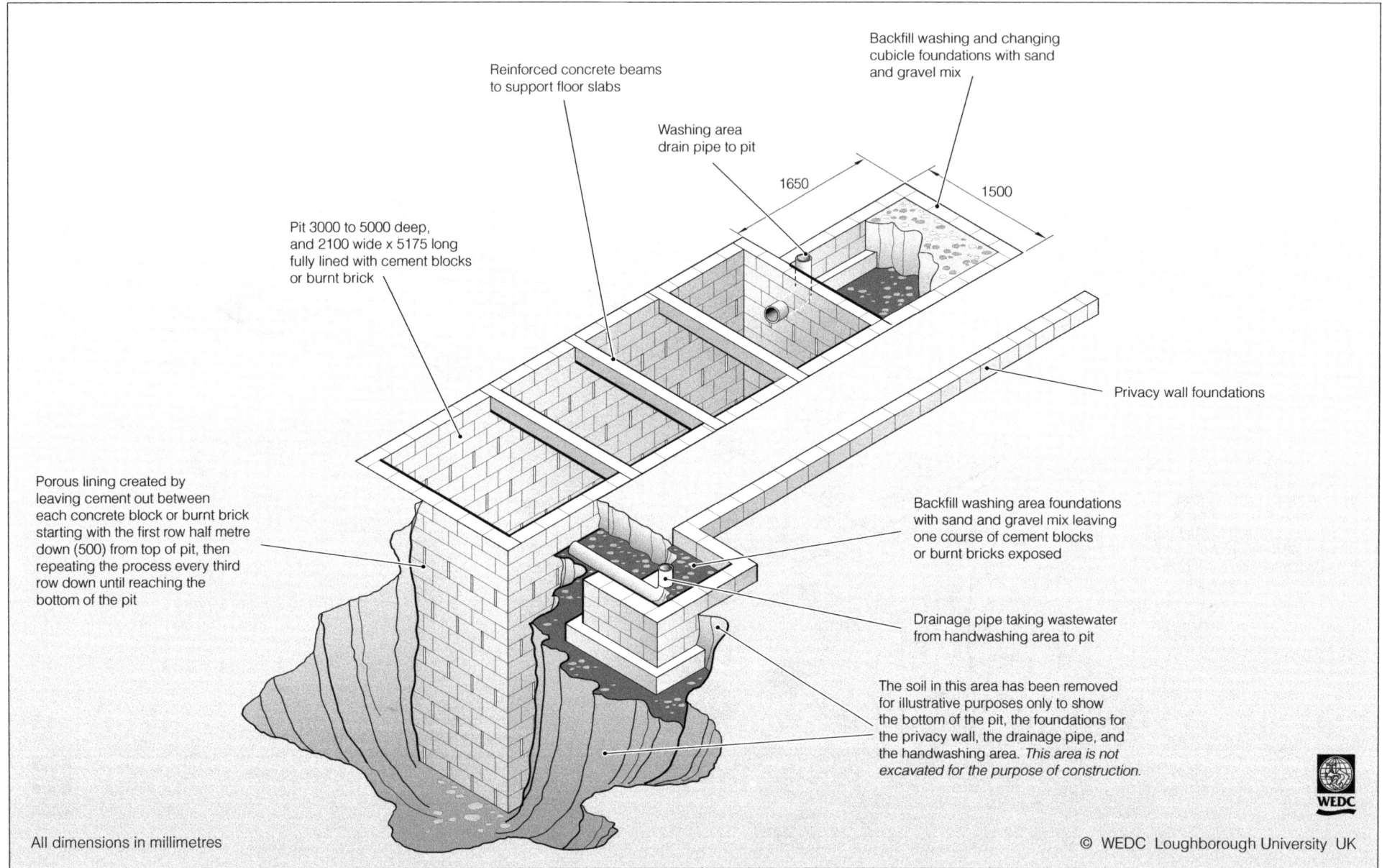

Guidelines

Reinforced concrete beams to support floor slabs

Backfill washing and changing cubicle foundations with sand and gravel mix

Washing area drain pipe to pit

1650

1500

Pit 3000 to 5000 deep, and 2100 wide x 5175 long fully lined with cement blocks or burnt brick

Privacy wall foundations

Porous lining created by leaving cement out between each concrete block or burnt brick starting with the first row half metre down (500) from top of pit, then repeating the process every third row down until reaching the bottom of the pit

Backfill washing area foundations with sand and gravel mix leaving one course of cement blocks or burnt bricks exposed

Drainage pipe taking wastewater from handwashing area to pit

The soil in this area has been removed for illustrative purposes only to show the bottom of the pit, the foundations for the privacy wall, the drainage pipe, and the handwashing area. *This area is not excavated for the purpose of construction.*

All dimensions in millimetres

WEDC

© WEDC Loughborough University UK

24

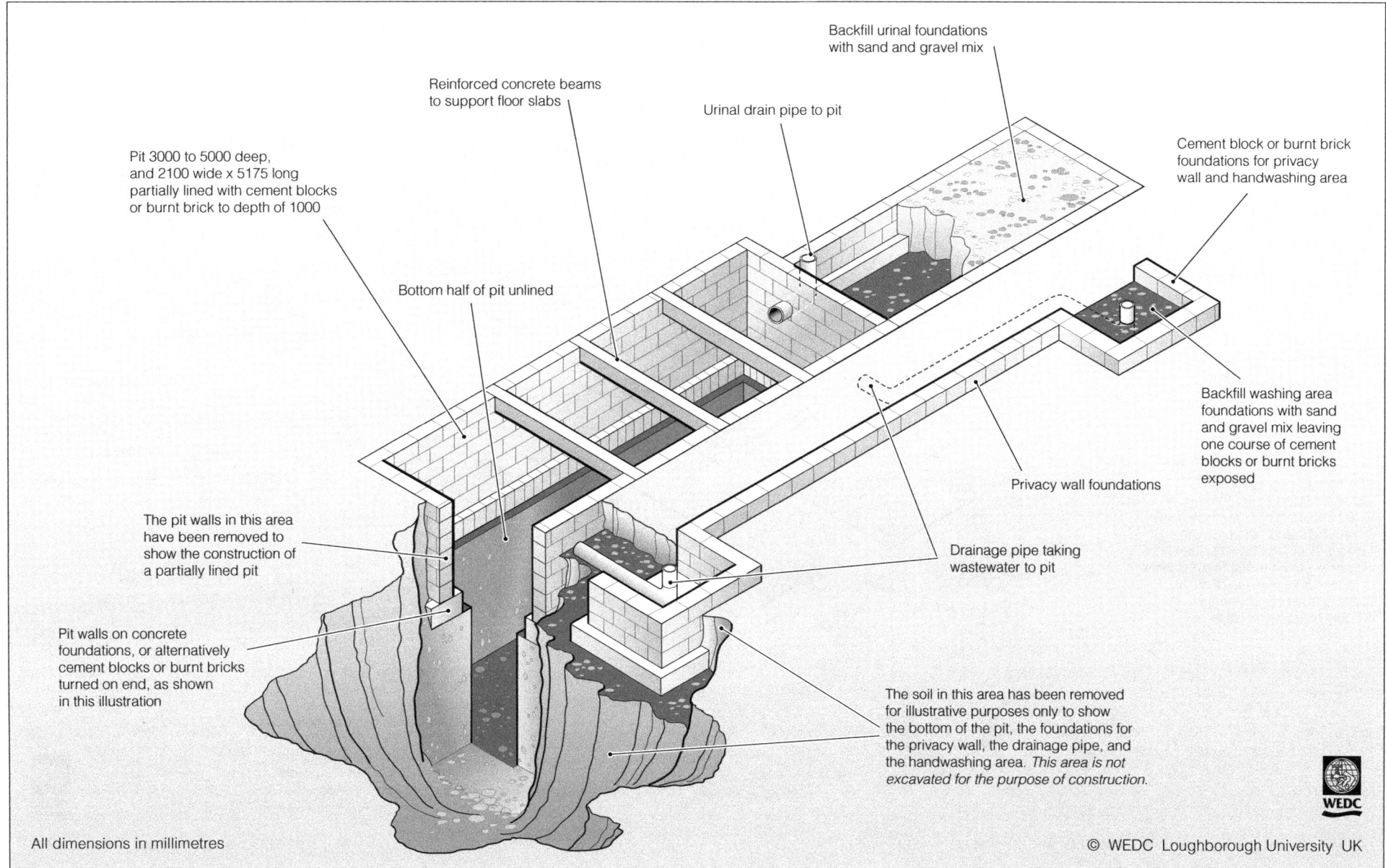

Backfill urinal foundations with sand and gravel mix

Reinforced concrete beams to support floor slabs

Urinal drain pipe to pit

Cement block or burnt brick foundations for privacy wall and handwashing area

Pit 3000 to 5000 deep, and 2100 wide x 5175 long partially lined with cement blocks or burnt brick to depth of 1000

Bottom half of pit unlined

The pit walls in this area have been removed to show the construction of a partially lined pit

Backfill washing area foundations with sand and gravel mix leaving one course of cement blocks or burnt bricks exposed

Privacy wall foundations

Pit walls on concrete foundations, or alternatively cement blocks or burnt bricks turned on end, as shown in this illustration

Drainage pipe taking wastewater to pit

The soil in this area has been removed for illustrative purposes only to show the bottom of the pit, the foundations for the privacy wall, the drainage pipe, and the handwashing area. *This area is not excavated for the purpose of construction.*

Guidelines

All dimensions in millimetres

WEDC

© WEDC Loughborough University UK

25

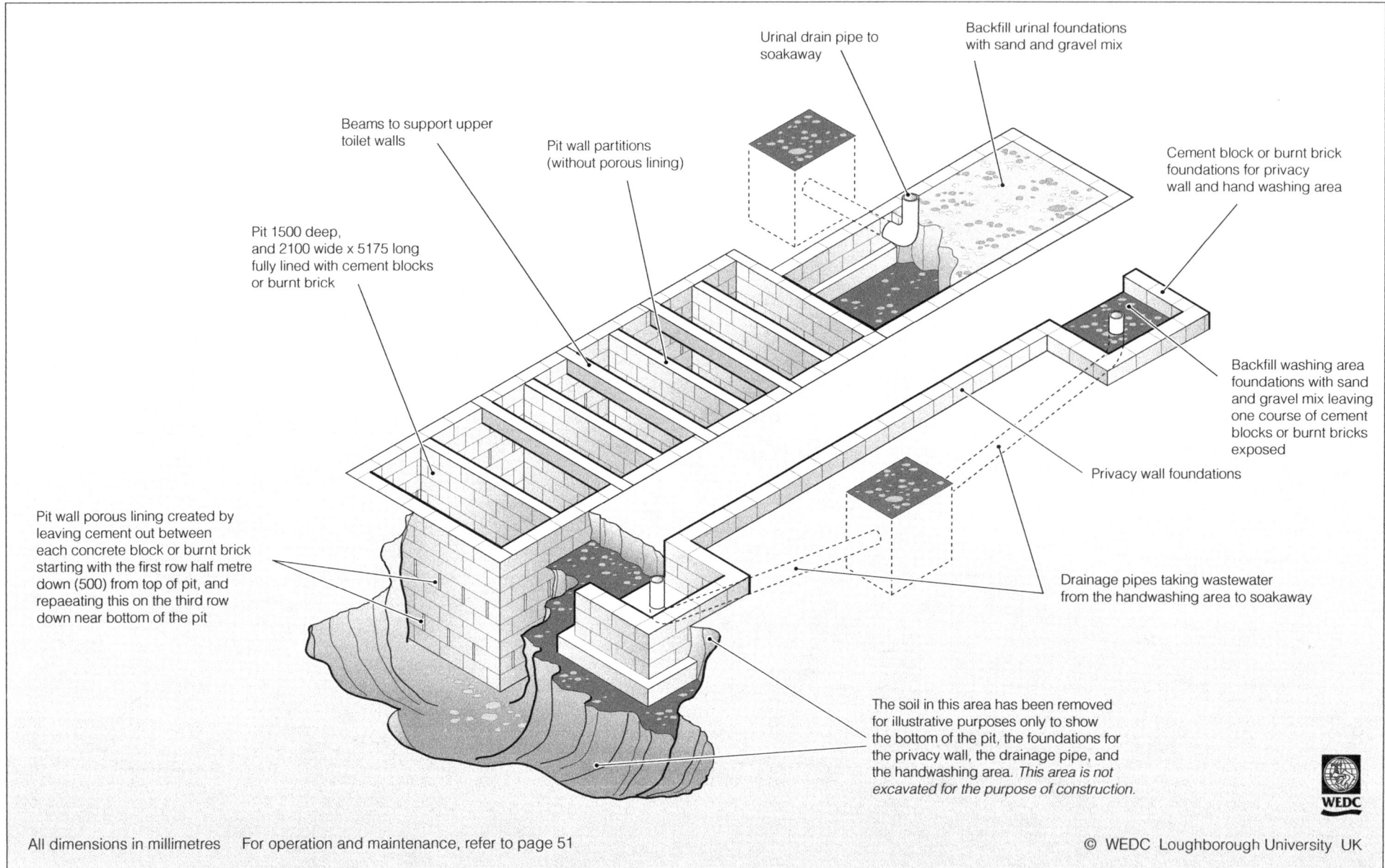

Guidelines

Urinal drain pipe to soakaway

Backfill urinal foundations with sand and gravel mix

Beams to support upper toilet walls

Pit wall partitions (without porous lining)

Cement block or burnt brick foundations for privacy wall and hand washing area

Pit 1500 deep, and 2100 wide x 5175 long fully lined with cement blocks or burnt brick

Backfill washing area foundations with sand and gravel mix leaving one course of cement blocks or burnt bricks exposed

Privacy wall foundations

Pit wall porous lining created by leaving cement out between each concrete block or burnt brick starting with the first row half metre down (500) from top of pit, and repaeating this on the third row down near bottom of the pit

Drainage pipes taking wastewater from the handwashing area to soakaway

The soil in this area has been removed for illustrative purposes only to show the bottom of the pit, the foundations for the privacy wall, the drainage pipe, and the handwashing area. *This area is not excavated for the purpose of construction.*

WEDC

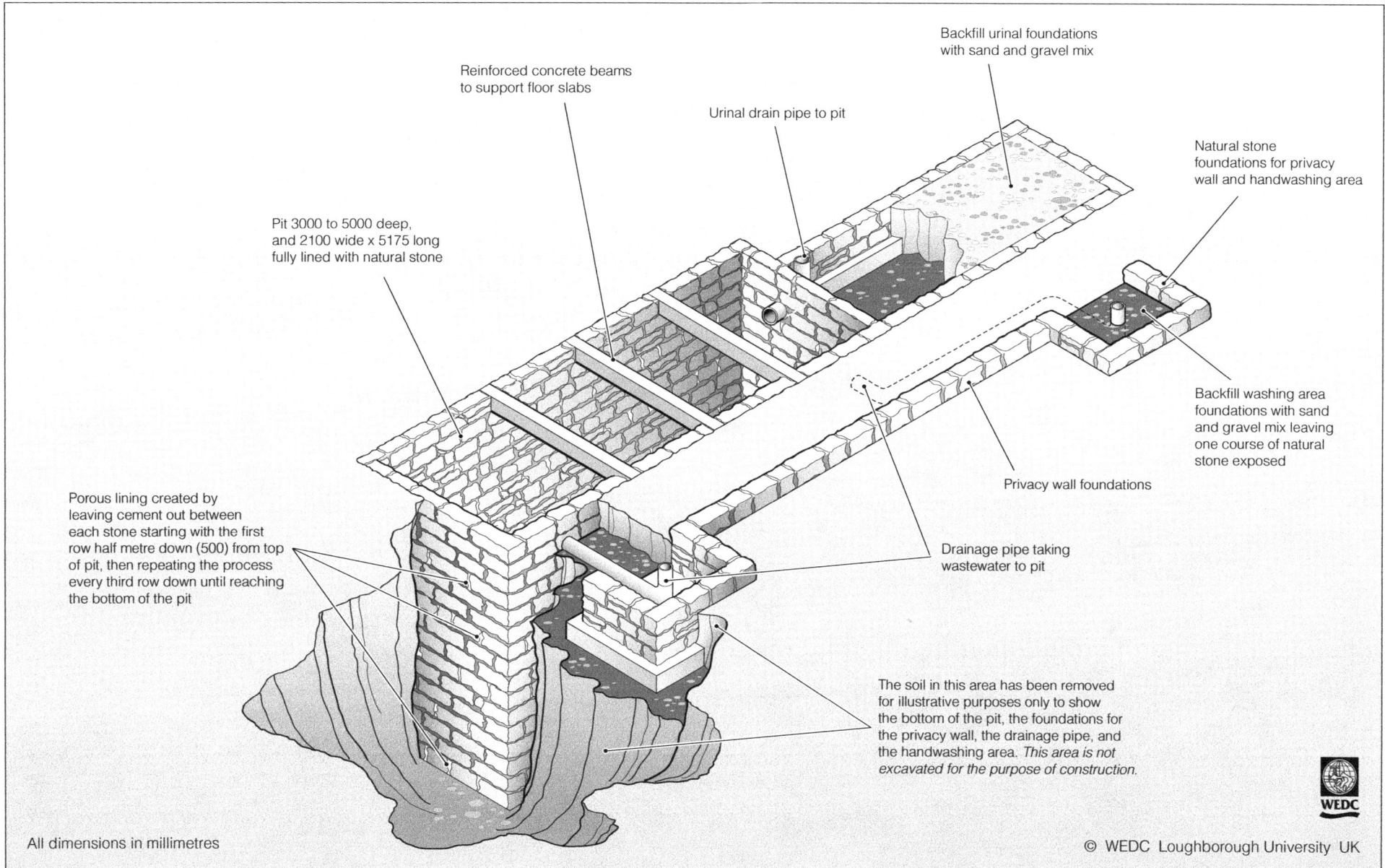

Guidelines

Backfill urinal foundations
with sand and gravel mix

Reinforced concrete beams
to support floor slabs

Urinal drain pipe to pit

Natural stone
foundations for privacy
wall and handwashing area

Pit 3000 to 5000 deep,
and 2100 wide x 5175 long
fully lined with natural stone

Backfill washing area
foundations with sand
and gravel mix leaving
one course of natural
stone exposed

Privacy wall foundations

Porous lining created by
leaving cement out between
each stone starting with the first
row half metre down (500) from top
of pit, then repeating the process
every third row down until reaching
the bottom of the pit

Drainage pipe taking
wastewater to pit

The soil in this area has been removed
for illustrative purposes only to show
the bottom of the pit, the foundations for
the privacy wall, the drainage pipe, and
the handwashing area. *This area is not
excavated for the purpose of construction.*

All dimensions in millimetres

WEDC

Guidelines

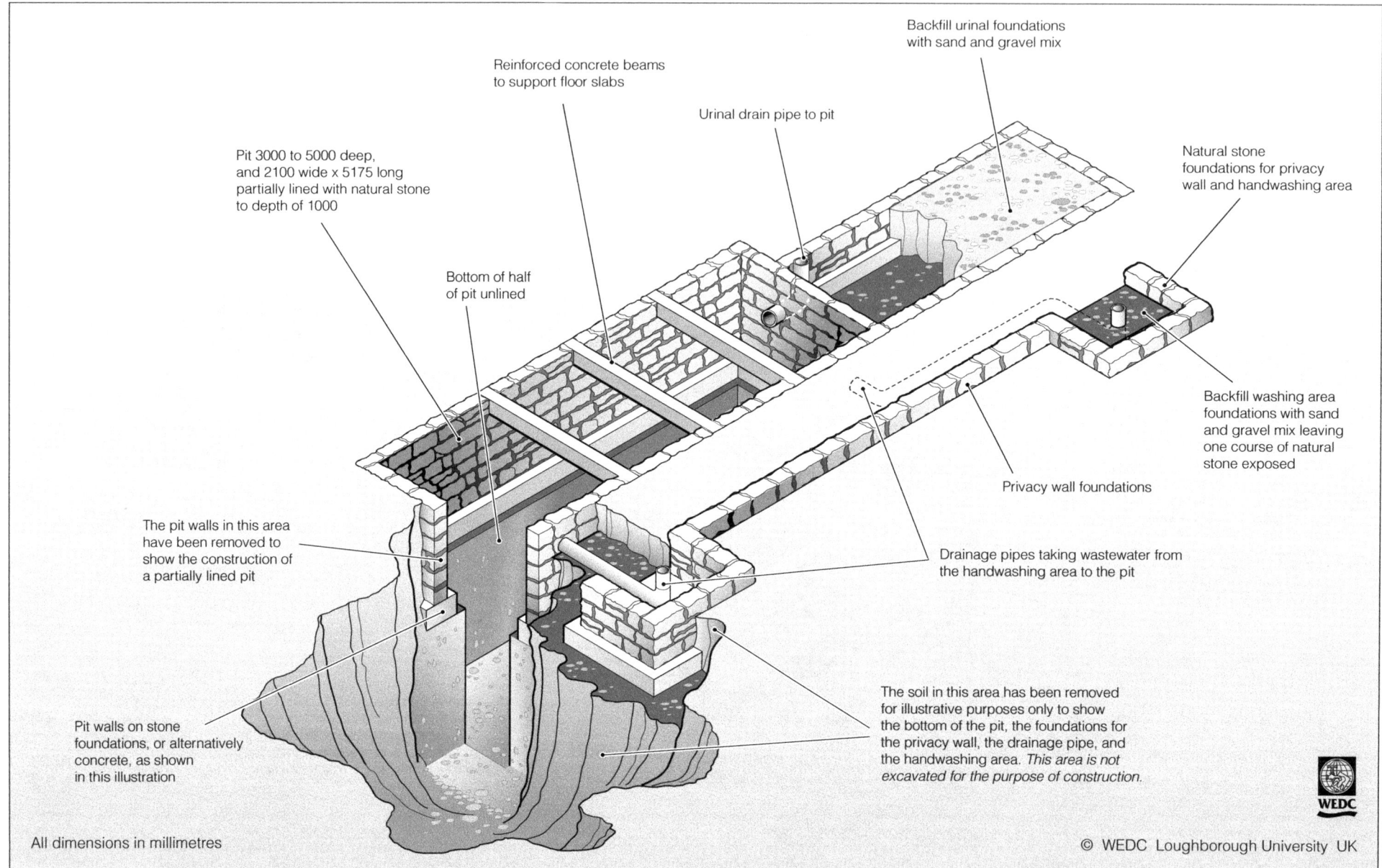

Backfill urinal foundations
with sand and gravel mix

Reinforced concrete beams
to support floor slabs

Urinal drain pipe to pit

Pit 3000 to 5000 deep,
and 2100 wide x 5175 long
partially lined with natural stone
to depth of 1000

Natural stone
foundations for privacy
wall and handwashing area

Bottom of half
of pit unlined

The pit walls in this area
have been removed to
show the construction of
a partially lined pit

Backfill washing area
foundations with sand
and gravel mix leaving
one course of natural
stone exposed

Privacy wall foundations

Drainage pipes taking wastewater from
the handwashing area to the pit

Pit walls on stone
foundations, or alternatively
concrete, as shown
in this illustration

The soil in this area has been removed
for illustrative purposes only to show
the bottom of the pit, the foundations for
the privacy wall, the drainage pipe, and
the handwashing area. *This area is not
excavated for the purpose of construction.*

All dimensions in millimetres

WEDC

© WEDC Loughborough University UK

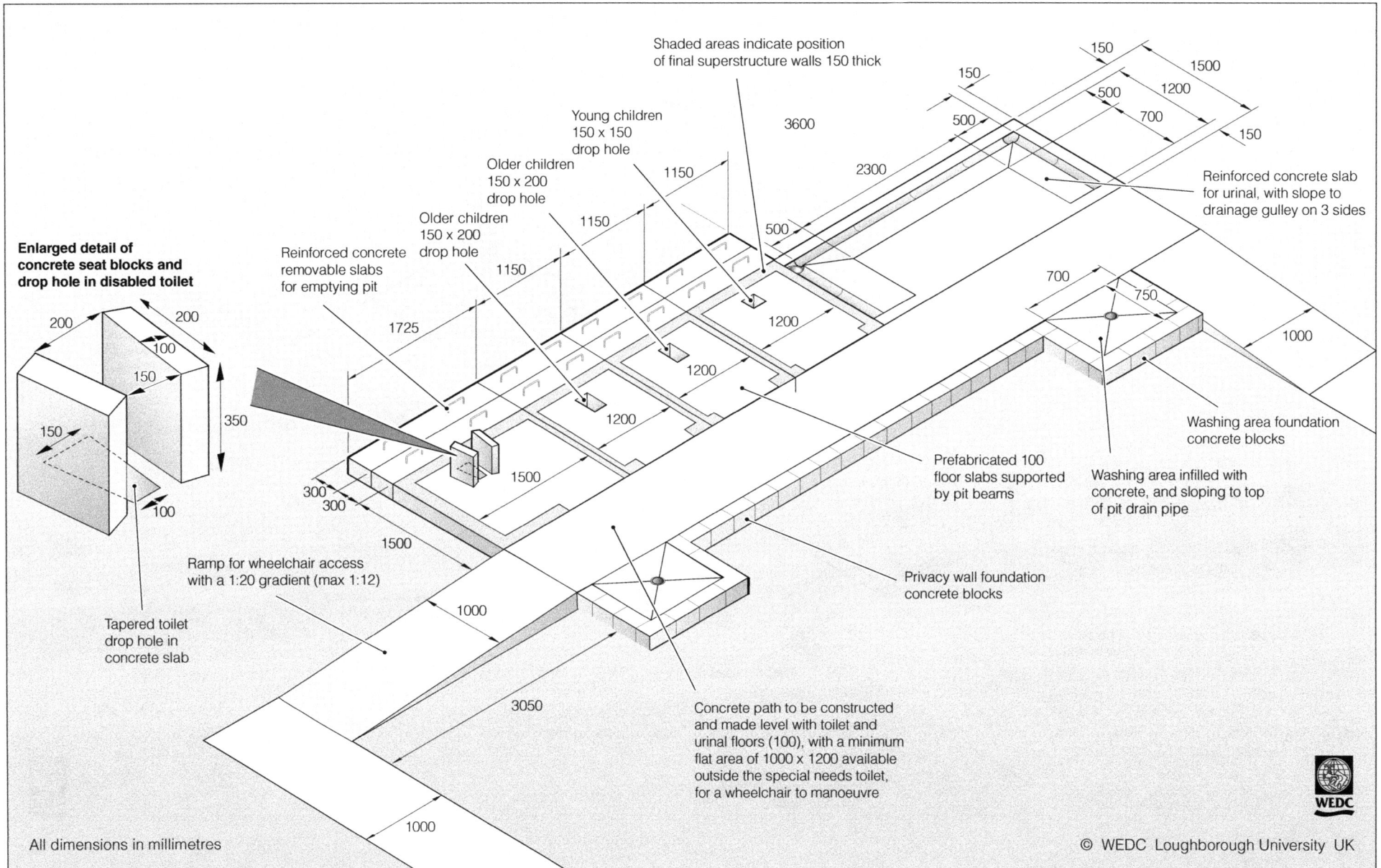

Shaded areas indicate position
of final superstructure walls 150 thick

Young children
150 x 150
drop hole

Older children
150 x 200
drop hole

Older children
150 x 200
drop hole

**Enlarged detail of
concrete seat blocks and
drop hole in disabled toilet**

Reinforced concrete
removable slabs
for emptying pit

Reinforced concrete slab
for urinal, with slope to
drainage gulley on 3 sides

150

1500

150

500

1200

700

150

3600

2300

1150

1150

1150

500

500

700

750

1000

200

200

100

150

350

150

100

1725

1200

1200

1200

1500

1500

Washing area foundation
concrete blocks

Washing area infilled with
concrete, and sloping to top
of pit drain pipe

Prefabricated 100
floor slabs supported
by pit beams

300
300

1500

Ramp for wheelchair access
with a 1:20 gradient (max 1:12)

Privacy wall foundation
concrete blocks

Tapered toilet
drop hole in
concrete slab

1000

3050

Concrete path to be constructed
and made level with toilet and
urinal floors (100), with a minimum
flat area of 1000 x 1200 available
outside the special needs toilet,
for a wheelchair to manoeuvre

1000

All dimensions in millimetres

Guidelines

WEDC

© WEDC Loughborough University UK

29

Figure 2.2. Cement block or burnt brick with concrete slab (girls)

Guidelines

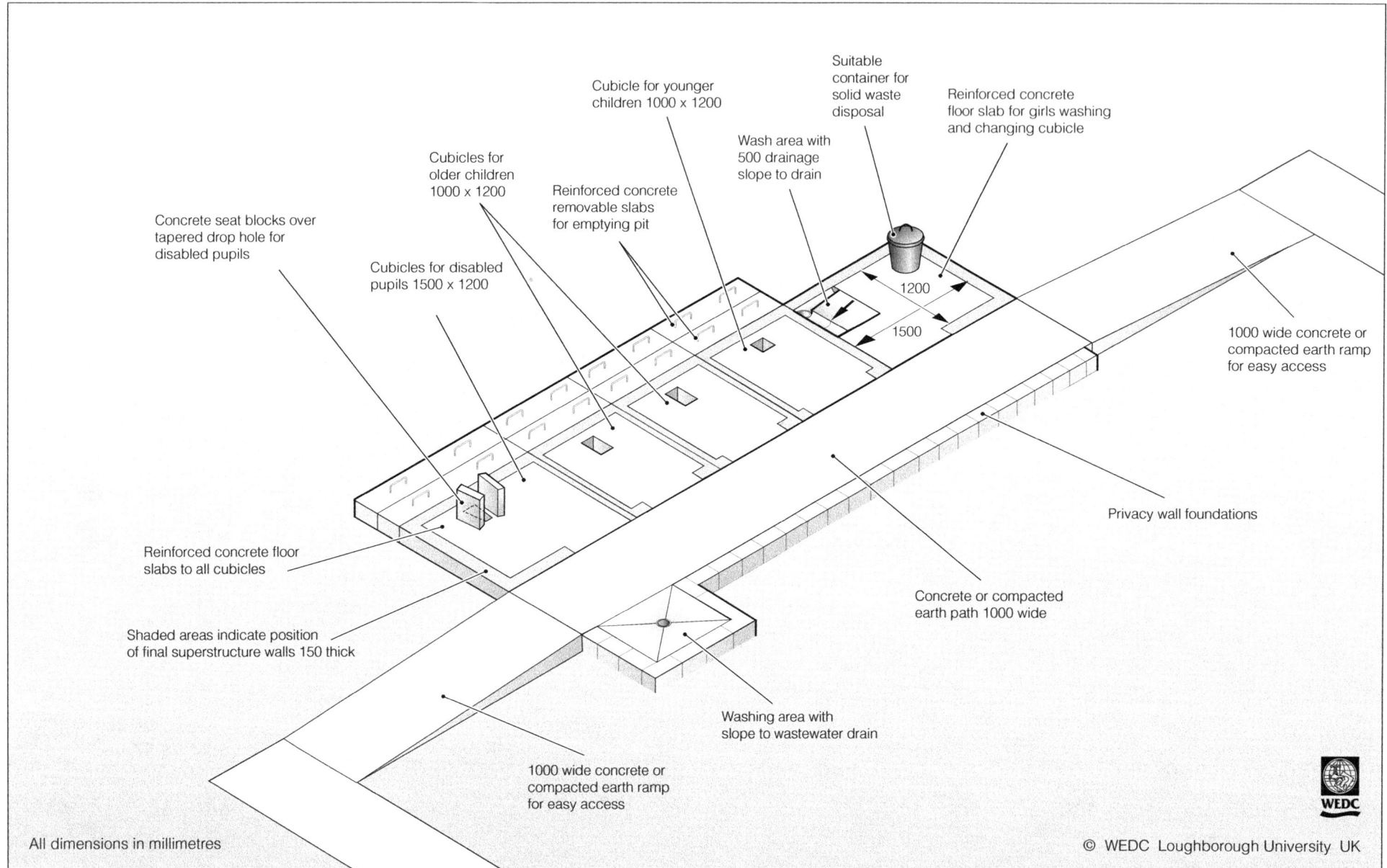

Suitable container for solid waste disposal

Cubicle for younger children 1000 x 1200

Reinforced concrete floor slab for girls washing and changing cubicle

Wash area with 500 drainage slope to drain

Cubicles for older children 1000 x 1200

Reinforced concrete removable slabs for emptying pit

Concrete seat blocks over tapered drop hole for disabled pupils

Cubicles for disabled pupils 1500 x 1200

1200

1500

1000 wide concrete or compacted earth ramp for easy access

Privacy wall foundations

Reinforced concrete floor slabs to all cubicles

Concrete or compacted earth path 1000 wide

Shaded areas indicate position of final superstructure walls 150 thick

Washing area with slope to wastewater drain

1000 wide concrete or compacted earth ramp for easy access

All dimensions in millimetres

© WEDC Loughborough University UK

30

Figure 2.3. Natural stone with concrete slab (boys)

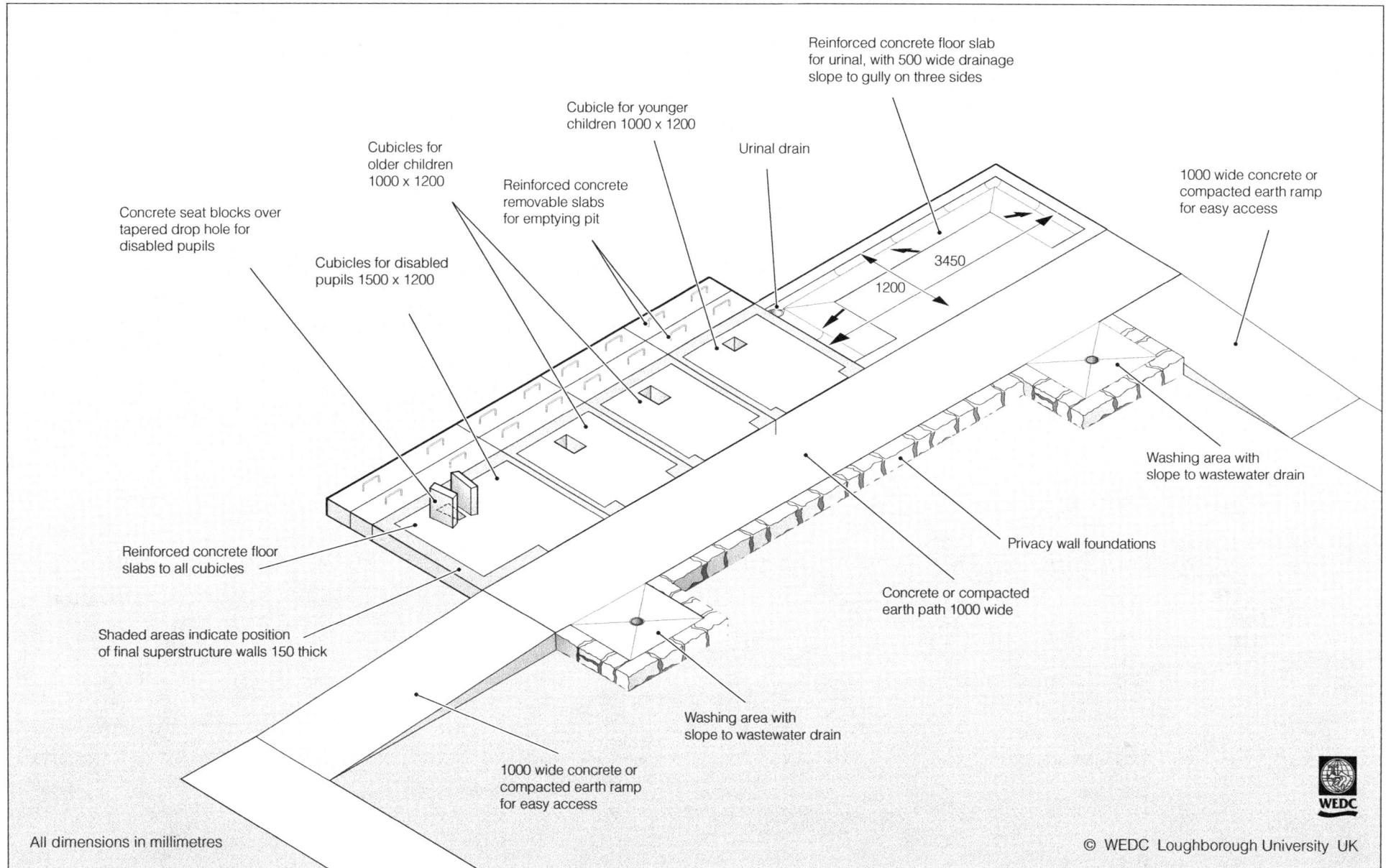

Reinforced concrete floor slab for urinal, with 500 wide drainage slope to gully on three sides

Cubicle for younger children 1000 x 1200

Urinal drain

Cubicles for older children 1000 x 1200

Reinforced concrete removable slabs for emptying pit

1000 wide concrete or compacted earth ramp for easy access

Concrete seat blocks over tapered drop hole for disabled pupils

Cubicles for disabled pupils 1500 x 1200

3450

1200

Washing area with slope to wastewater drain

Privacy wall foundations

Reinforced concrete floor slabs to all cubicles

Concrete or compacted earth path 1000 wide

Shaded areas indicate position of final superstructure walls 150 thick

Washing area with slope to wastewater drain

1000 wide concrete or compacted earth ramp for easy access

All dimensions in millimetres

© WEDC Loughborough University UK

Guidelines

WEDC

Guidelines

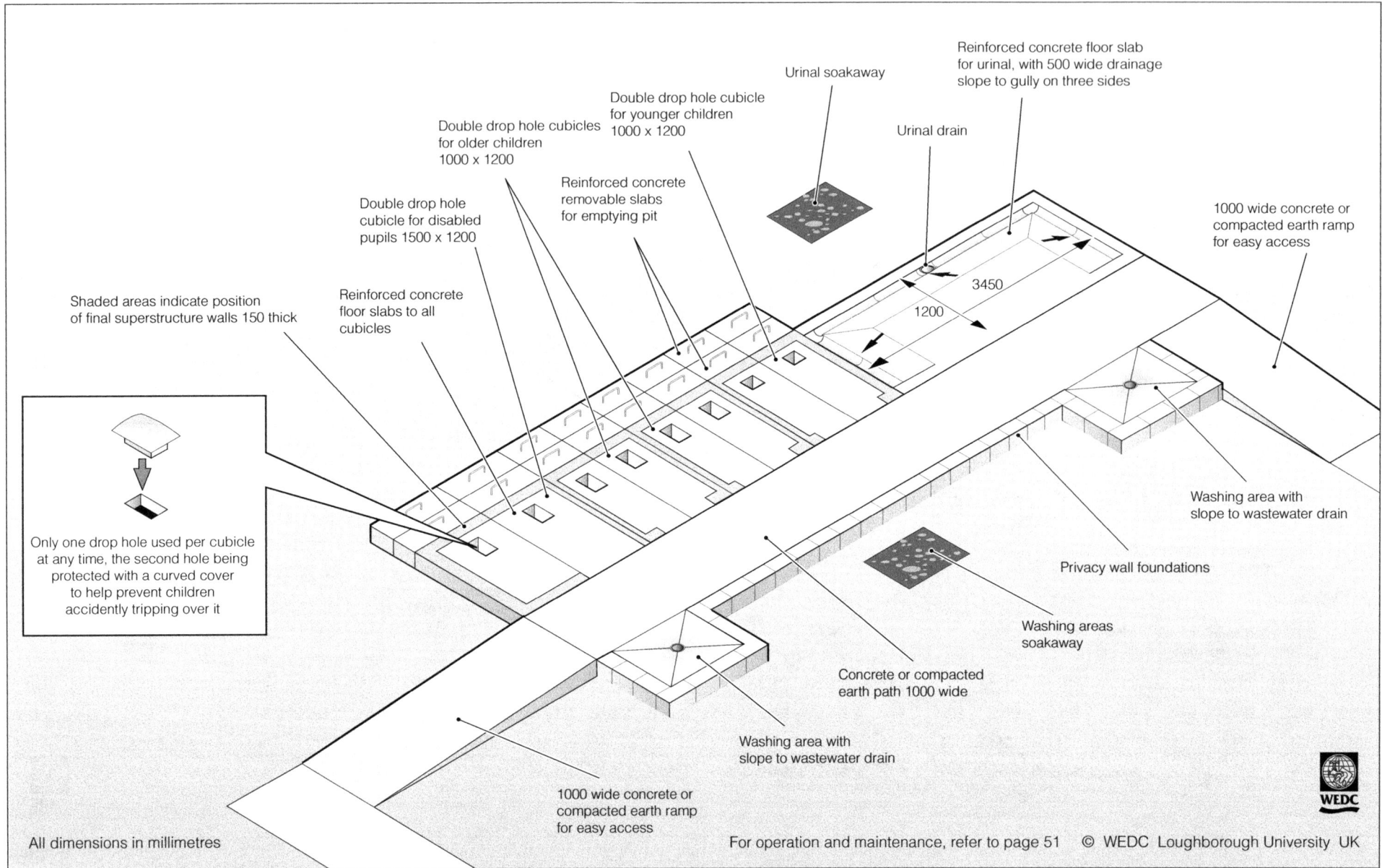

Reinforced concrete floor slab for urinal, with 500 wide drainage slope to gully on three sides

Urinal soakaway

Urinal drain

Double drop hole cubicle for younger children 1000 x 1200

Double drop hole cubicles for older children 1000 x 1200

Reinforced concrete removable slabs for emptying pit

Double drop hole cubicle for disabled pupils 1500 x 1200

Shaded areas indicate position of final superstructure walls 150 thick

Reinforced concrete floor slabs to all cubicles

1000 wide concrete or compacted earth ramp for easy access

3450

1200

Washing area with slope to wastewater drain

Privacy wall foundations

Only one drop hole used per cubicle at any time, the second hole being protected with a curved cover to help prevent children accidently tripping over it

Washing areas soakaway

Concrete or compacted earth path 1000 wide

Washing area with slope to wastewater drain

1000 wide concrete or compacted earth ramp for easy access

All dimensions in millimetres

For operation and maintenance, refer to page 51   © WEDC Loughborough University UK

WEDC

32

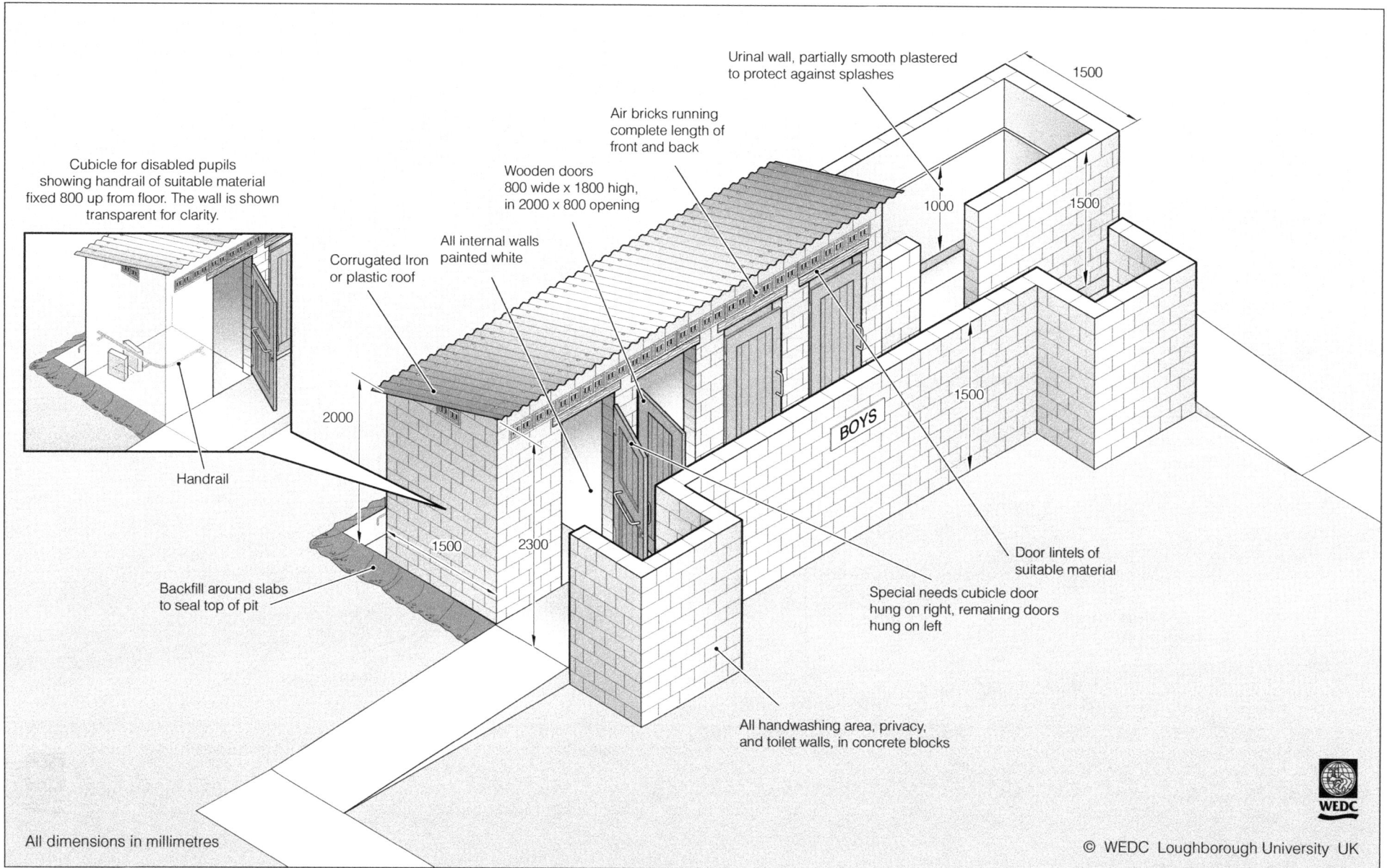

Cubicle for disabled pupils showing handrail of suitable material fixed 800 up from floor. The wall is shown transparent for clarity.

Handrail

Backfill around slabs to seal top of pit

Corrugated Iron or plastic roof

All internal walls painted white

Wooden doors 800 wide x 1800 high, in 2000 x 800 opening

Air bricks running complete length of front and back

Urinal wall, partially smooth plastered to protect against splashes

2000

1500

2300

1000

1500

1500

1500

BOYS

Door lintels of suitable material

Special needs cubicle door hung on right, remaining doors hung on left

All handwashing area, privacy, and toilet walls, in concrete blocks

Guidelines

All dimensions in millimetres

© WEDC Loughborough University UK

WEDC

33

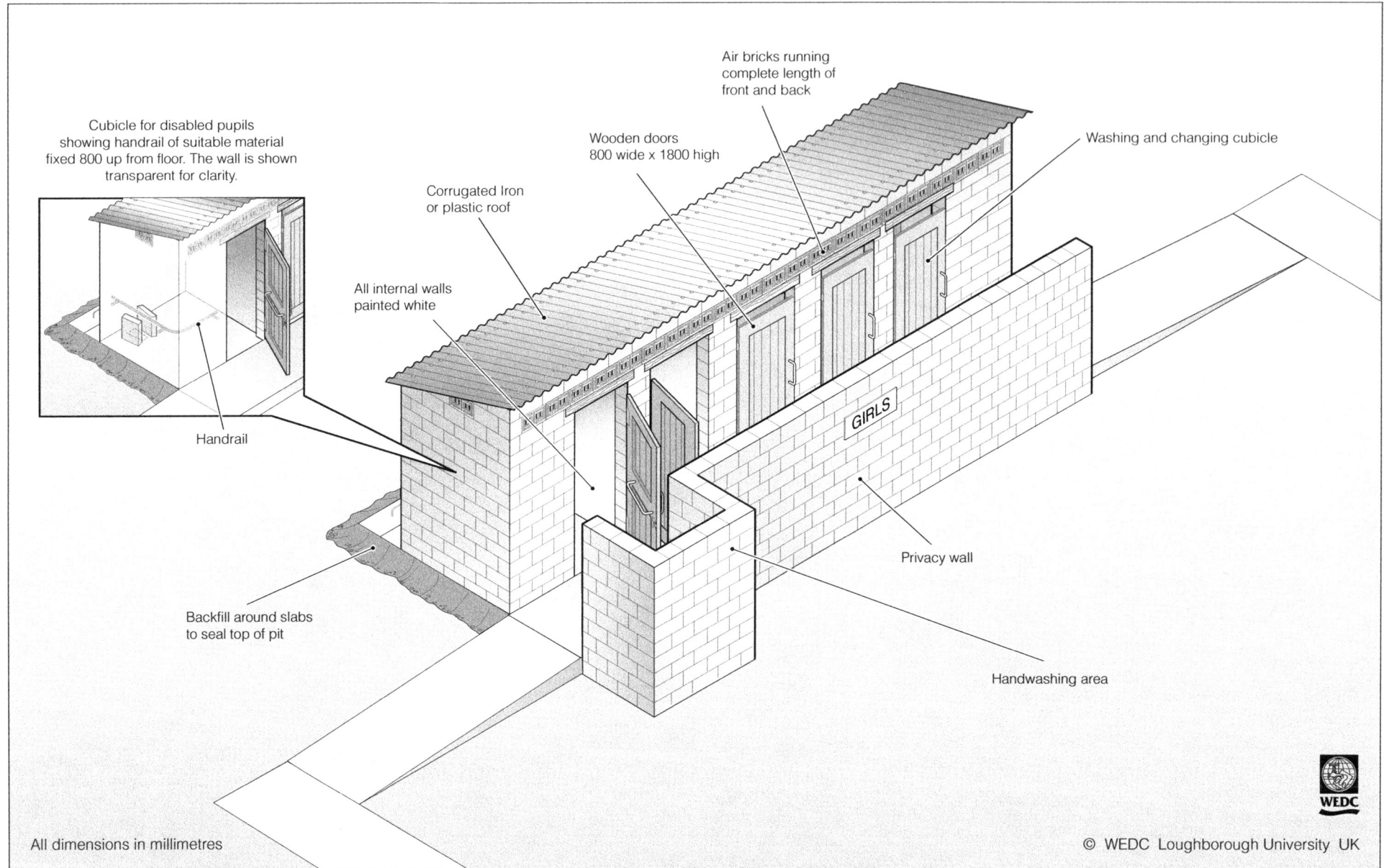

Cubicle for disabled pupils showing handrail of suitable material fixed 800 up from floor. The wall is shown transparent for clarity.

Air bricks running complete length of front and back

Wooden doors 800 wide x 1800 high

Washing and changing cubicle

Corrugated Iron or plastic roof

All internal walls painted white

Handrail

GIRLS

Backfill around slabs to seal top of pit

Privacy wall

Handwashing area

All dimensions in millimetres

© WEDC Loughborough University UK

WEDC

34

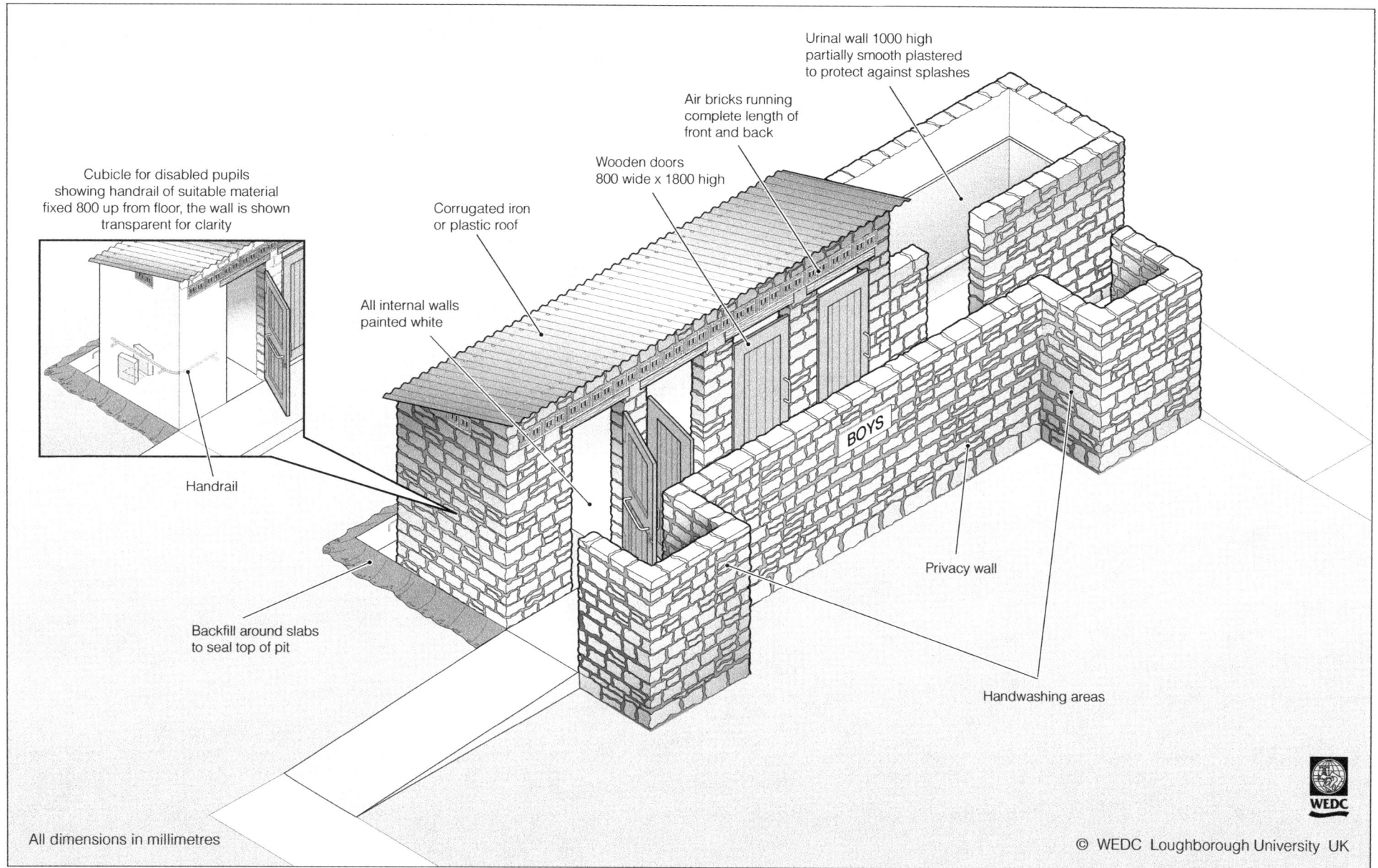

Figure 3.3. Natural stone superstructure (boys)

Guidelines

Urinal wall 1000 high
partially smooth plastered
to protect against splashes

Air bricks running
complete length of
front and back

Wooden doors
800 wide x 1800 high

Cubicle for disabled pupils
showing handrail of suitable material
fixed 800 up from floor, the wall is shown
transparent for clarity

Corrugated iron
or plastic roof

All internal walls
painted white

Handrail

BOYS

Privacy wall

Backfill around slabs
to seal top of pit

Handwashing areas

All dimensions in millimetres

© WEDC Loughborough University UK

WEDC

Guidelines

Urinal wall 1000 high partially smooth plastered to protect against splashes

Chicken mesh on wood frame air vents, running complete length of front and back

Corrugated iron doors on wooden frame 800 wide x 1800 high

Cubicle for disabled pupils showing handrail of suitable material fixed 800 up from floor. The wall is shown transparent for clarity.

Corrugated iron or plastic roof

All internal walls painted white

BOYS

Handrail

Privacy wall

Backfill around slabs to seal top of pit

All walls corrugated iron on timber framewok

Handwashing areas

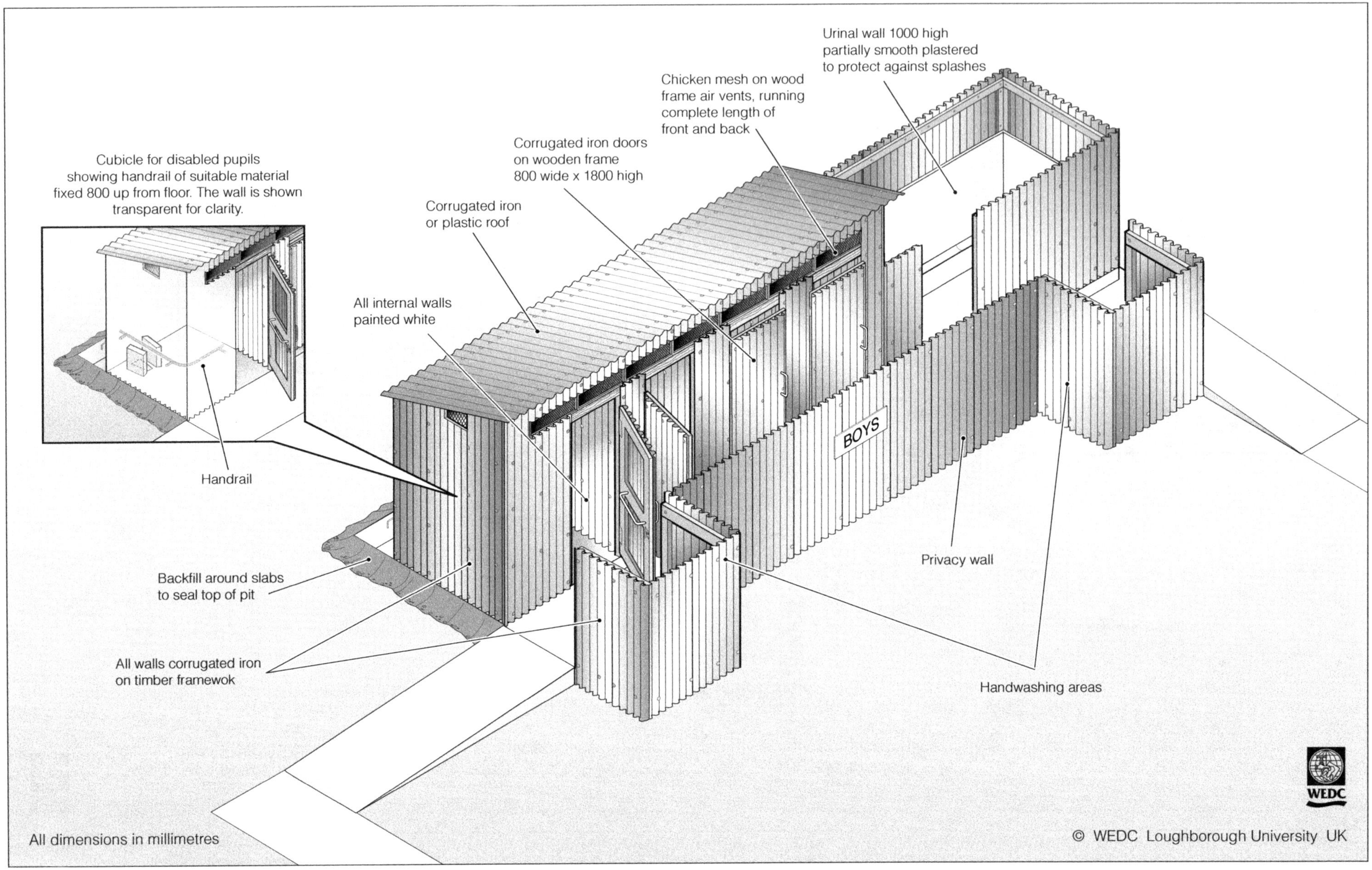

All dimensions in millimetres

© WEDC Loughborough University UK

WEDC

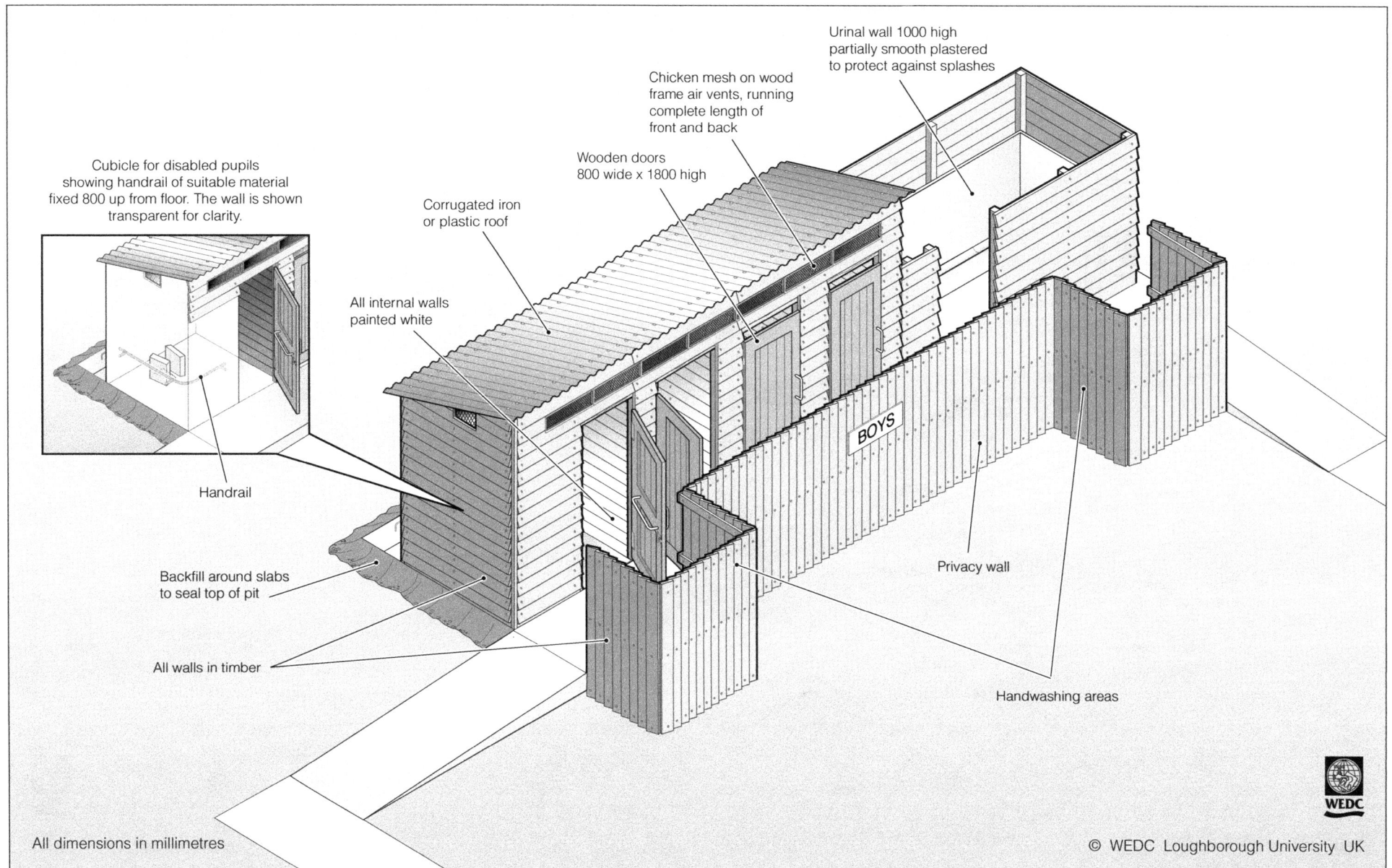

Guidelines

Urinal wall 1000 high
partially smooth plastered
to protect against splashes

Chicken mesh on wood
frame air vents, running
complete length of
front and back

Wooden doors
800 wide x 1800 high

Cubicle for disabled pupils
showing handrail of suitable material
fixed 800 up from floor. The wall is shown
transparent for clarity.

Corrugated iron
or plastic roof

All internal walls
painted white

BOYS

Handrail

Privacy wall

Backfill around slabs
to seal top of pit

Handwashing areas

All walls in timber

All dimensions in millimetres

© WEDC Loughborough University UK

WEDC

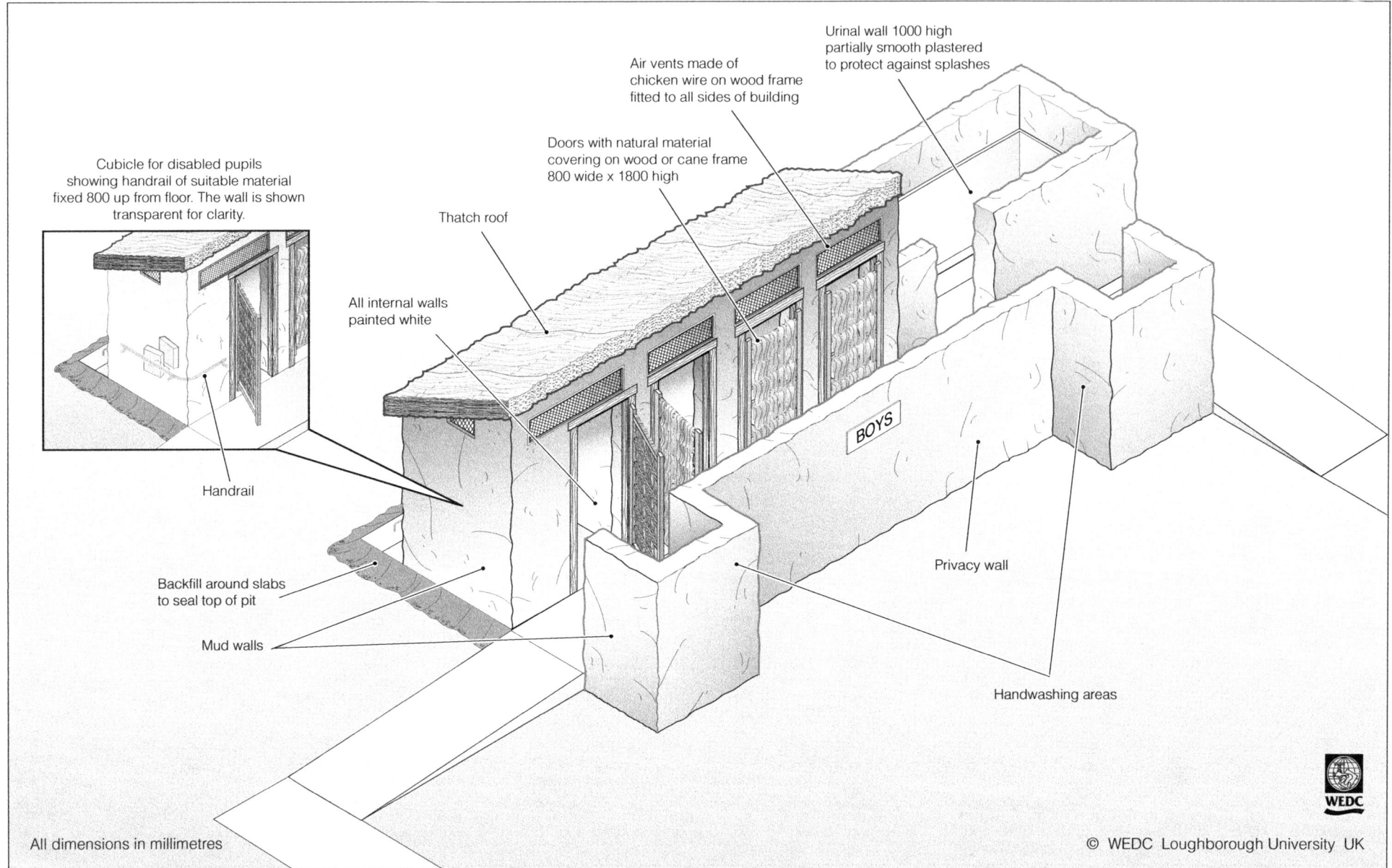

Urinal wall 1000 high
partially smooth plastered
to protect against splashes

Air vents made of
chicken wire on wood frame
fitted to all sides of building

Doors with natural material
covering on wood or cane frame
800 wide x 1800 high

Cubicle for disabled pupils
showing handrail of suitable material
fixed 800 up from floor. The wall is shown
transparent for clarity.

Thatch roof

All internal walls
painted white

BOYS

Handrail

Backfill around slabs
to seal top of pit

Mud walls

Privacy wall

Handwashing areas

All dimensions in millimetres

WEDC

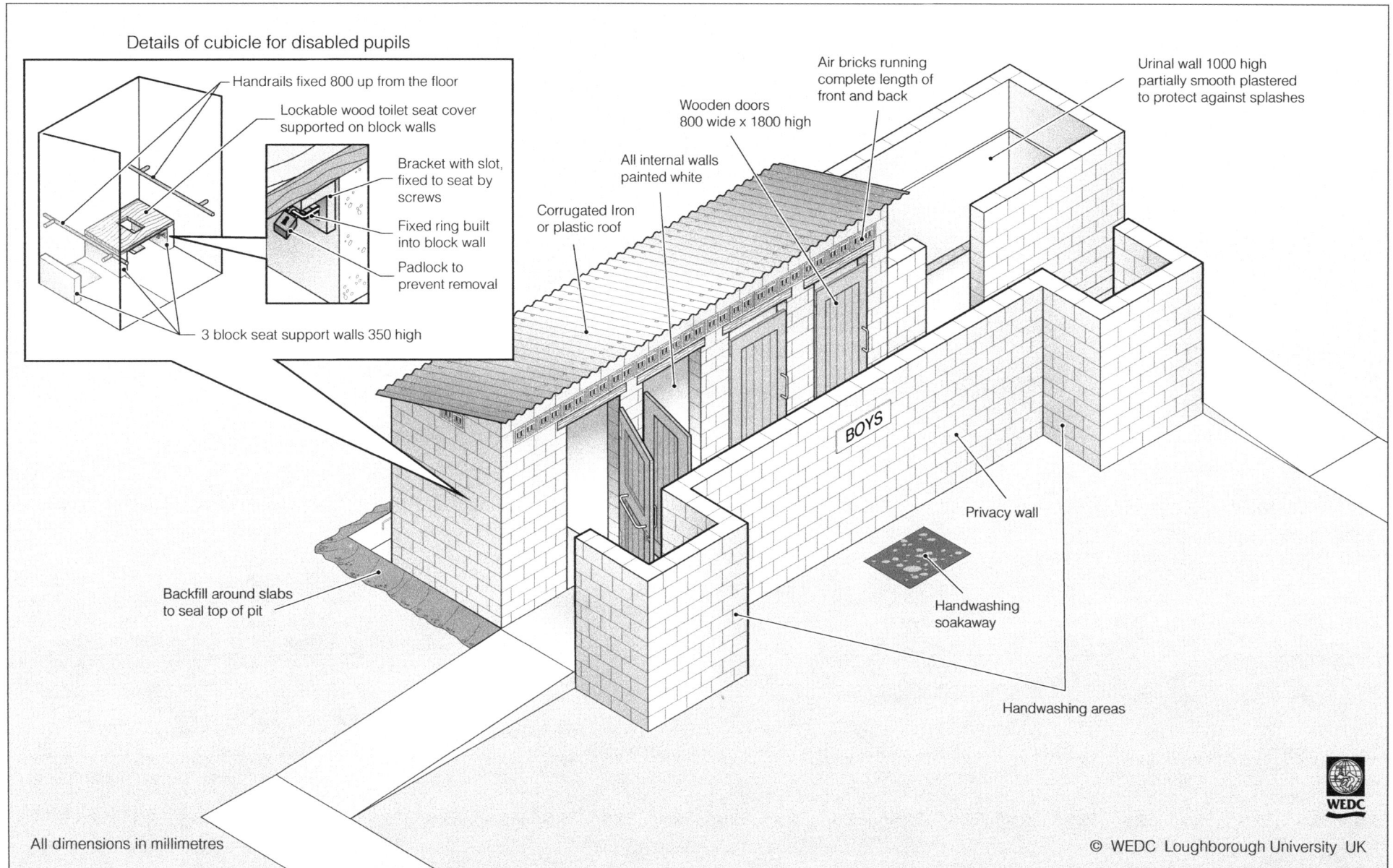

Details of cubicle for disabled pupils

Handrails fixed 800 up from the floor

Lockable wood toilet seat cover supported on block walls

Bracket with slot, fixed to seat by screws

Fixed ring built into block wall

Padlock to prevent removal

3 block seat support walls 350 high

Air bricks running complete length of front and back

Urinal wall 1000 high partially smooth plastered to protect against splashes

Wooden doors 800 wide x 1800 high

All internal walls painted white

Corrugated Iron or plastic roof

BOYS

Privacy wall

Handwashing soakaway

Backfill around slabs to seal top of pit

Handwashing areas

All dimensions in millimetres

WEDC

© WEDC Loughborough University UK

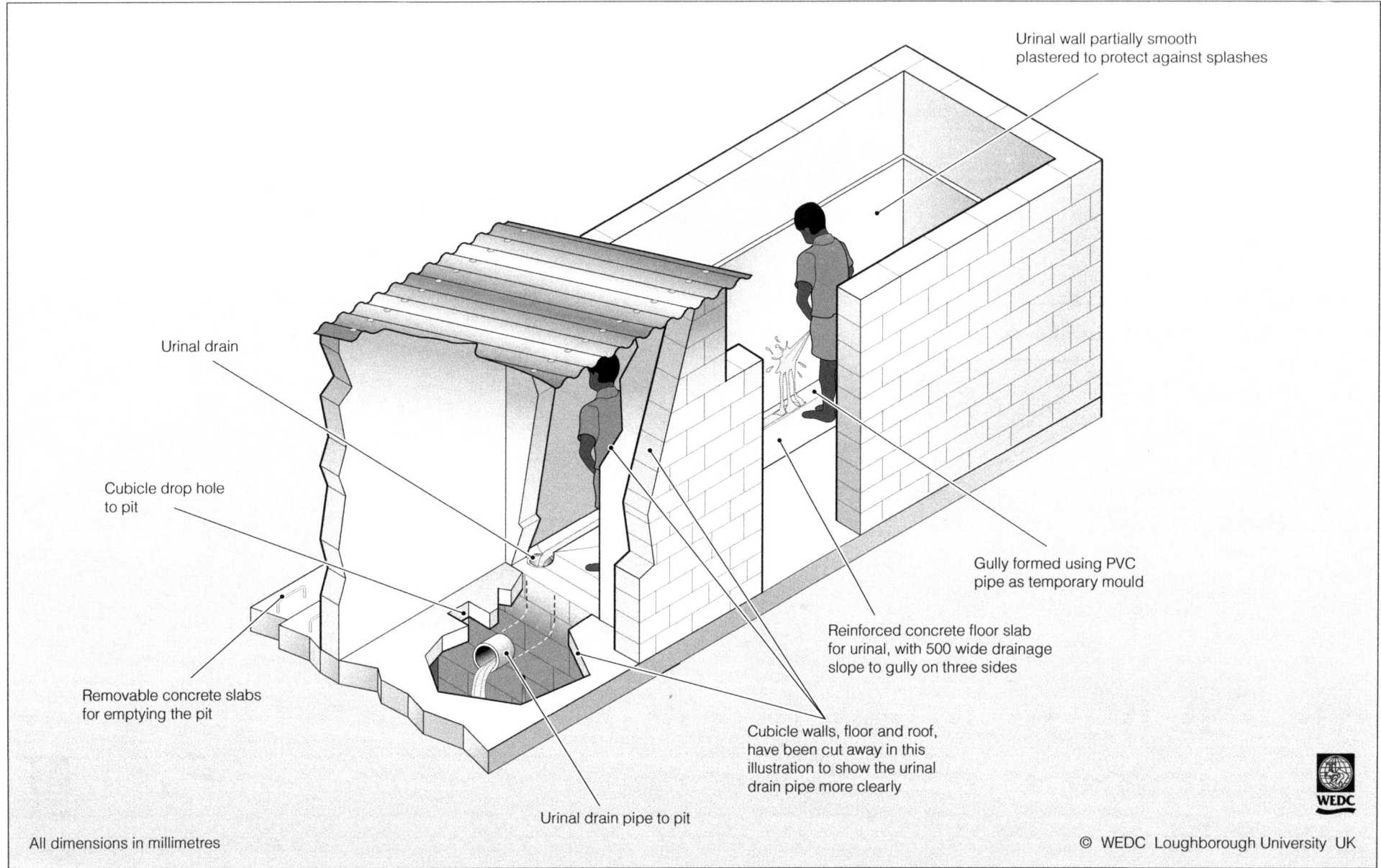

Urinal wall partially smooth
plastered to protect against splashes

Urinal drain

Cubicle drop hole
to pit

Gully formed using PVC
pipe as temporary mould

Reinforced concrete floor slab
for urinal, with 500 wide drainage
slope to gully on three sides

Removable concrete slabs
for emptying the pit

Cubicle walls, floor and roof,
have been cut away in this
illustration to show the urinal
drain pipe more clearly

Urinal drain pipe to pit

All dimensions in millimetres

© WEDC Loughborough University UK

WEDC

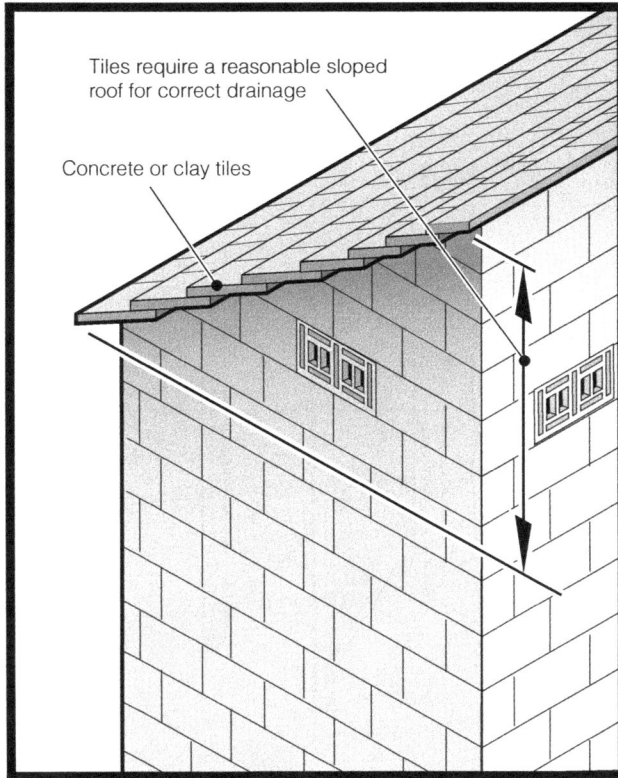

Concrete or clay tiles

To ensure correct drainage, tiled roofs require a reasonable sloped roof, which in turn will mean a higher front wall. In addition, tiles require suitable rafters and battens for attachment. All this places considerable extra weight on the supporting walls and therefore makes tiles more suitable for fixing to cement block, burnt brick or stone superstructues.

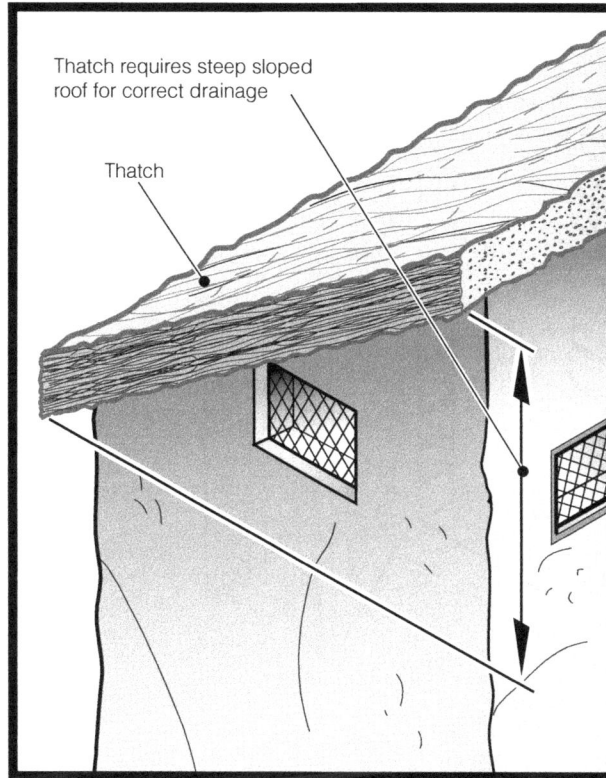

Thatch

Thatch requires a steeper sloped roof for correct drainage and subsequently a higher front wall to accommodate this, but does have the advantage that the roof can be made from local natural materials. Its light construction makes it particulary suitable for non load-bearing structures such as mud buildings.

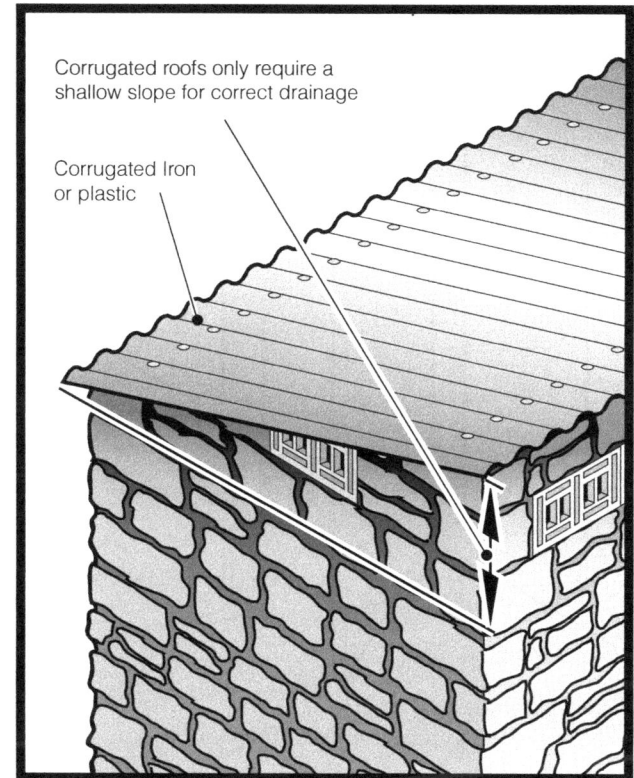

Corrugated iron or plastic

Corrugated iron is a versatile roofing material which only requires a shallow slope for drainage. It is also available in lightweight plastic which has the added advantage that it will not rust. Corrugated roofs are therefore suitable for most superstructures.

Figure 4.2. Alternative door materials

Guidelines

Timber

Wooden plank facing mounted on hinged wood frame 800mm wide x 1800mm high, complete with door furniture consisting of exterior door handle, internal closing bar, and door bolt for privacy.

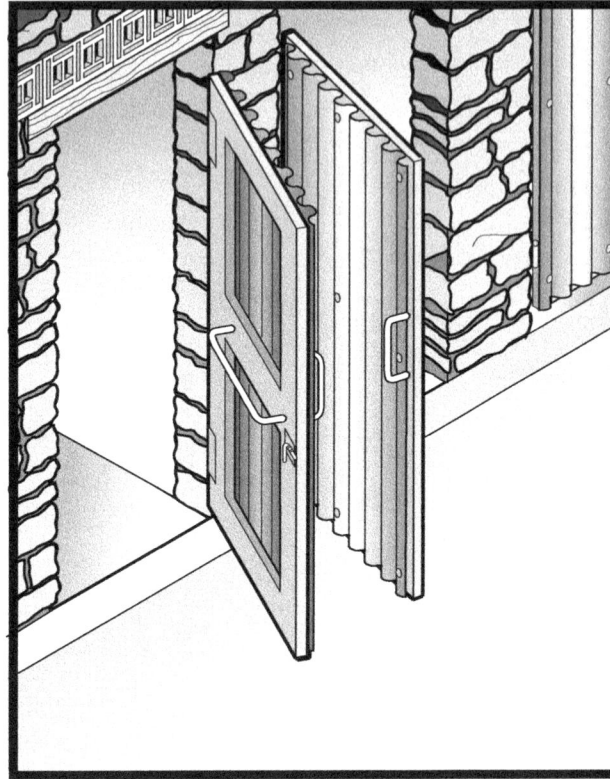

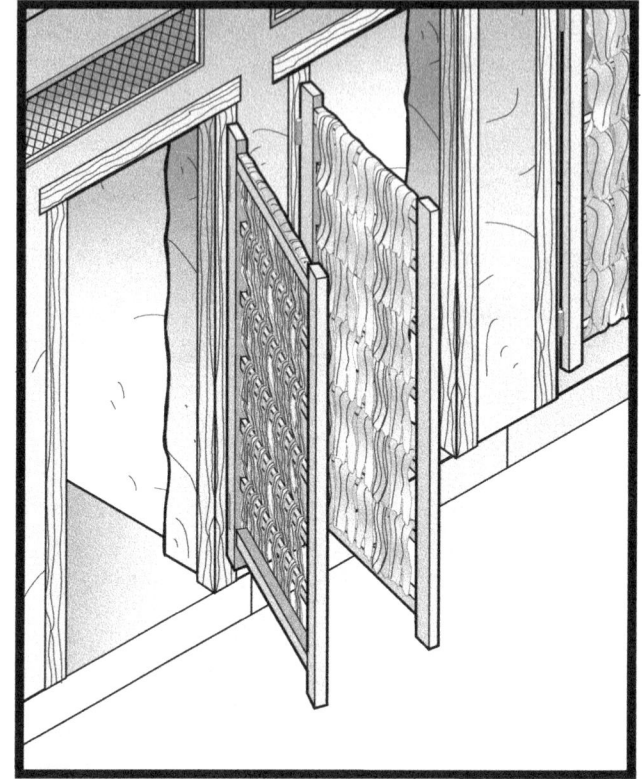

Corrugated iron

Corrugated iron facing mounted on hinged wood frame 800mm wide x 1800mm high complete with door furniture consisting of exterior door handle, internal closing bar, and door bolt for privacy.

Natural materials

Palm leaves or similar local materials interwoven on bamboo or timber hinged frame 800mm wide x 1800mm high.

© WEDC Loughborough University UK

Figure 5.1. Tipping containers for handwashing

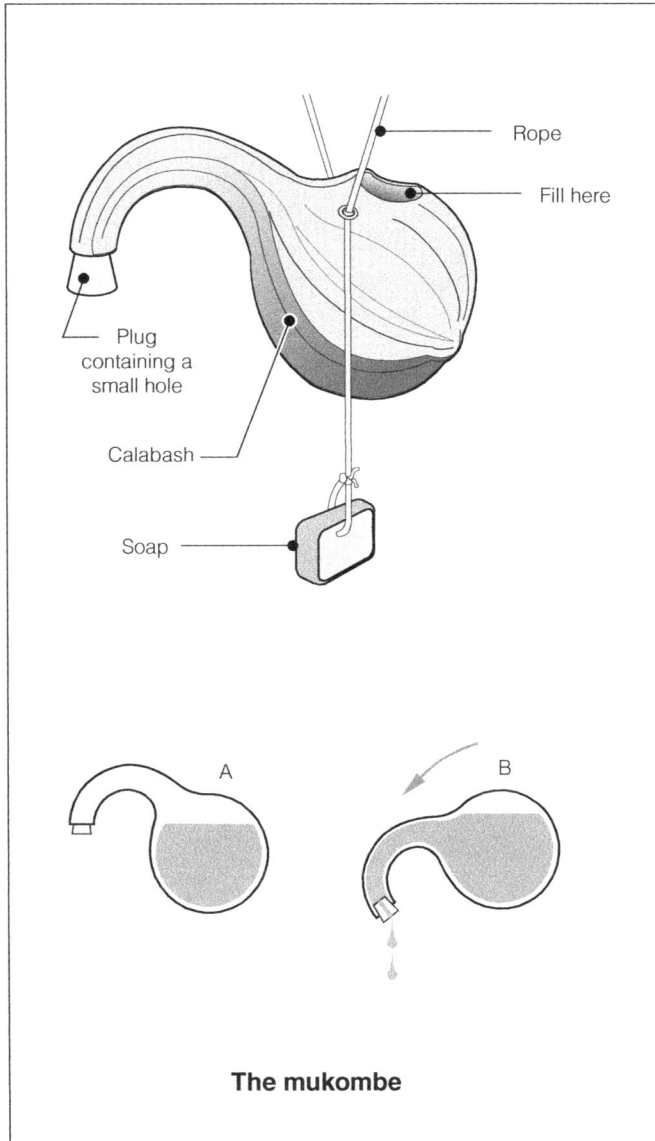

The mukombe

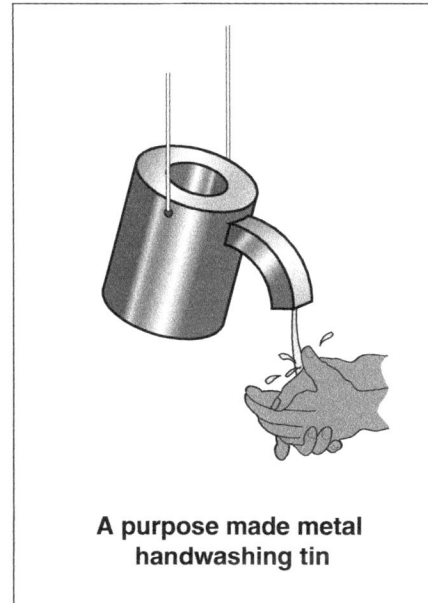

A purpose made metal handwashing tin

How to make a handwashing bottle
Choose a plastic bottle with a hollow handle. Heat the base of the handle with a candle flame until the plastic softens (1). Squeeze the plastic closed at this spot. Use a hot nail to make a hole above this spot (2). Make two holes at the same level on the opposite side of the bottle (3). Use string to hang the bottle from these holes (4).

Fill the bottle three-quarters full with clean water. Put the cap back on. Tip the bottle so that the hollow handle fills with water (see insert picture). Let the bottle swing back. The water in the handle will continue to run out of the small hole long enough for handwashing.

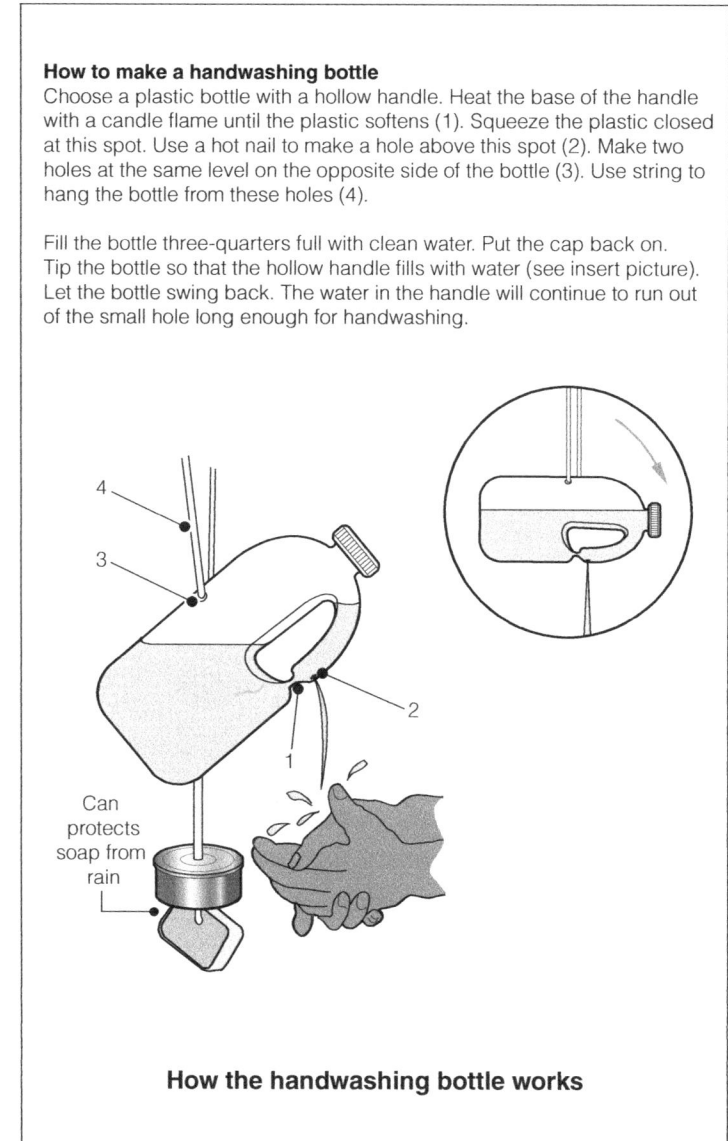

How the handwashing bottle works

Guidelines

43

Figure 5.2. Rainwater collection and standpost design

Guidelines

Downpipe drain
to remove debris

Both gutters drain
to down pipes

Water fills down pipe
and overlows to tank

5000 litre water tank

Tap

Wheelchair access ramp

All dimensions in millimetres

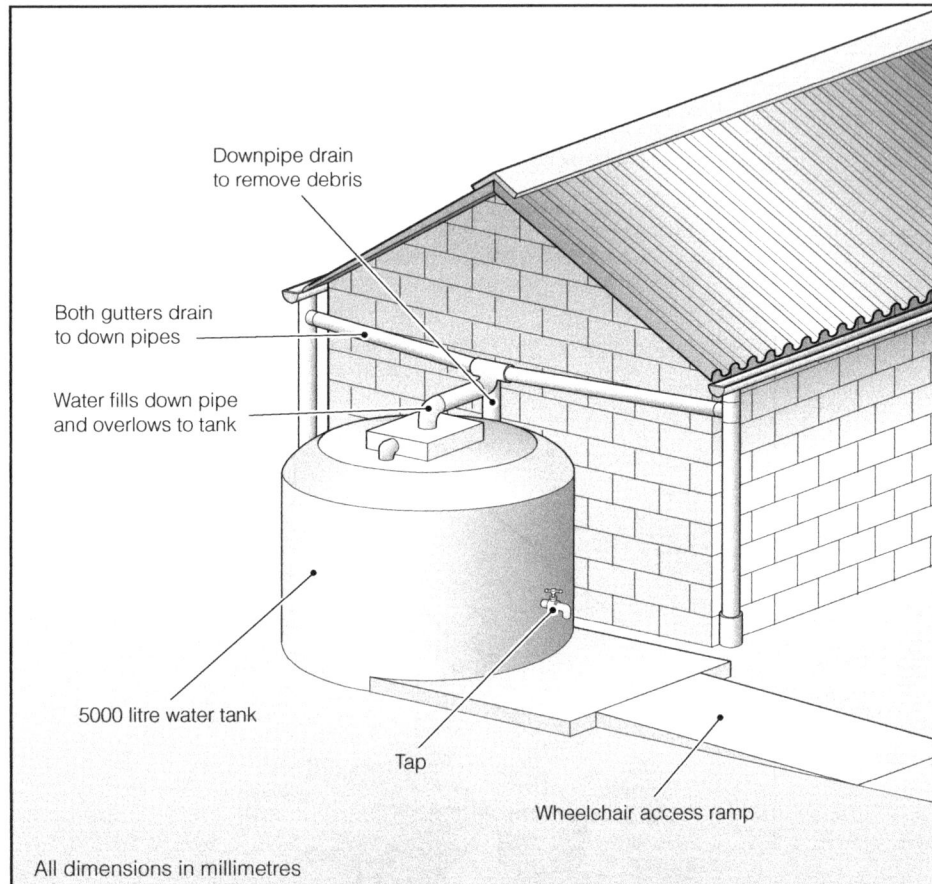

Rainwater collection

20mm tap, embedded in
standpost down centre of
plinth to a depth of 1100
for stability

Concrete apron 3000 x 1600,
with 1:50 fall on 4 sides down
to centre drain channel

Tap

400   400

1000

500 variable

400

800

100

1500

1600

Wastewater gulley
to drain or soakaway

All dimensions in millimetres

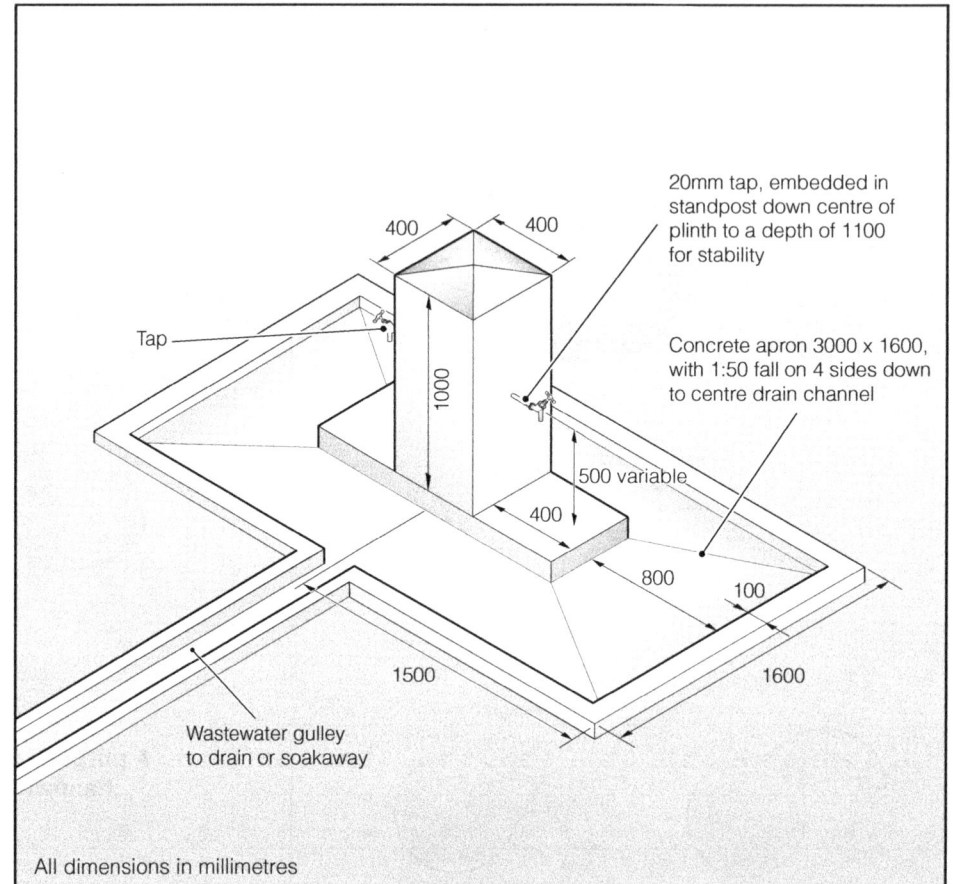

Dual tap standpost

Figure 5.3. Handpump and well designs

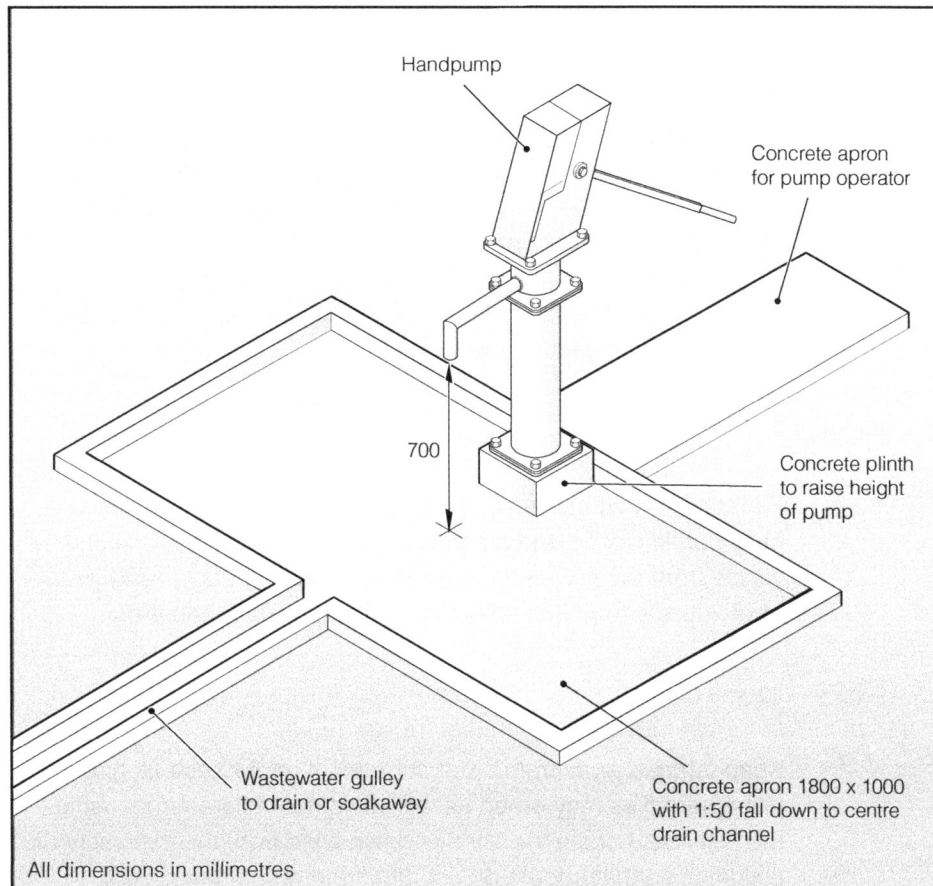

Handpump

Concrete apron for pump operator

Concrete plinth to raise height of pump

700

Wastewater gulley to drain or soakaway

Concrete apron 1800 x 1000 with 1:50 fall down to centre drain channel

All dimensions in millimetres

Handpump

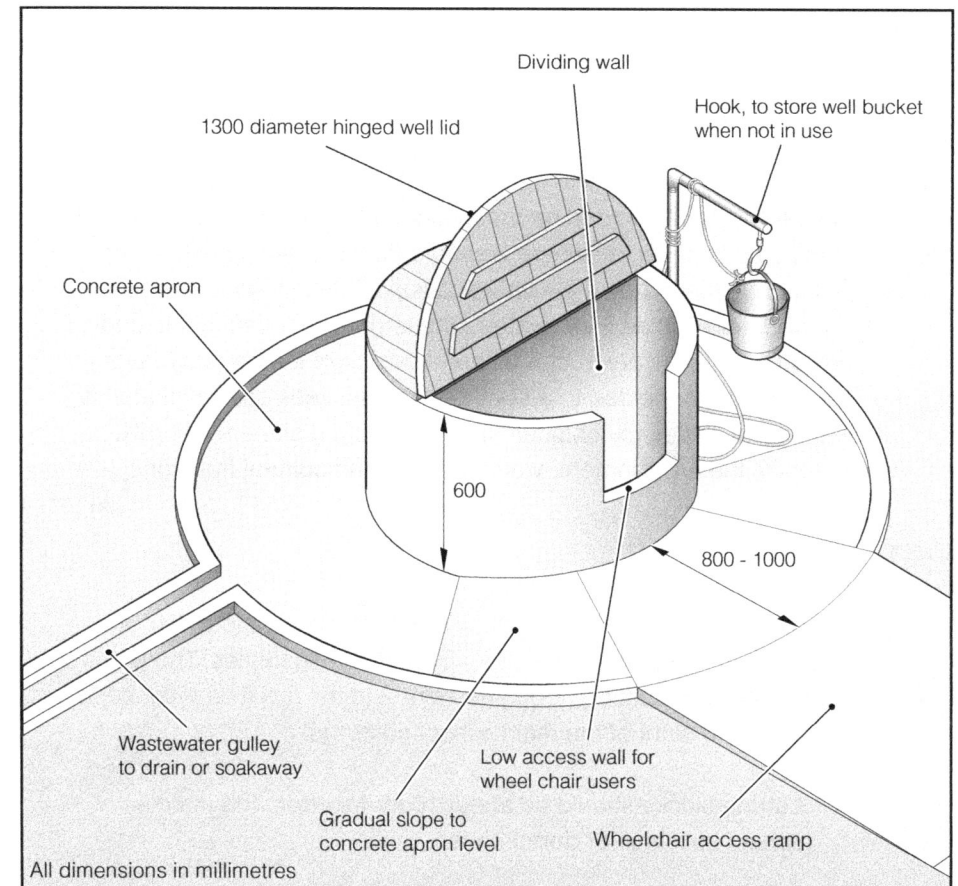

Dividing wall

1300 diameter hinged well lid

Hook, to store well bucket when not in use

Concrete apron

600

800 - 1000

Wastewater gulley to drain or soakaway

Low access wall for wheel chair users

Gradual slope to concrete apron level

Wheelchair access ramp

All dimensions in millimetres

Well

All dimensions in millimetres

Guidelines

Guidelines for siting school latrines

Where to build the latrines

Once you have decided on the design of the new latrine block, the next step is to decide where it should be built. Siting the latrine block will depend on the local conditions. The following guidelines should help you as they relate to the latrines pictured in this book. If you decide to construct a different design of latrine (such as a toilet block connected to a sewer) you must seek specialist advice. The main issues to consider when choosing a site are security, privacy, the environment, water, access and cultural traditions.

Security

Children have to feel safe when visiting latrines, without fear of harassment by people or attacks by animals or snakes. The paths to the latrines must be open and clear and the facilities must be in hearing and sight of the main school buildings.

- Latrine blocks should be about 10 metres from the main school buildings or dormitories.

- Blocks for boys and girls should be separated by about 10 metres to reduce the possibility of harassment.

- Latrine blocks should be sited away from the school boundary. The latrine doors should face towards the main school buildings.

Latrine blocks are vulnerable to vandalism and theft. If possible, ensure that the school compound is properly fenced to keep outsiders out. If this is not possible, fit all latrine cubicles with strong doors and securely lock them at night.

Latrines and latrine paths used by children living in dormitories must be illuminated at night.

Privacy

Facilities should guarantee privacy. Locate latrines away from busy public places and roads while ensuring that they are clearly visible from the main school buildings. Separate boys' and girls' blocks, preferably with some form of screen between them.

The environment

Keep latrines away from other sources of odour such as garbage pits where flies may breed as this will deter children from using the facilities. Locate the latrines down wind from the main school buildings so that odours do not affect the rest of the school.

Water

Latrines can contaminate nearby groundwater, so locate them at least 15 metres from wells and boreholes on the downhill side. Keep latrines 15 metres from any surface water such as ponds, rivers and streams.

Surface water can seriously damage latrine structures. Make sure that rainwater can drain away quickly and that surface water running across the site after heavy rain is diverted away from the latrine block.

Access

Latrine blocks must be connected to other school buildings by clearly defined paths. Paths must be wide enough for two people to pass each other, have an even surface and be self-draining. Steps may be necessary in steeply sloping areas but provide an alternative route using ramps for people with walking difficulties.

Cultural traditions

The religious or cultural traditions of some communities may also have a bearing on the siting and alignment of latrines. It is always important to consider such traditions before finally deciding where to locate the latrine block.

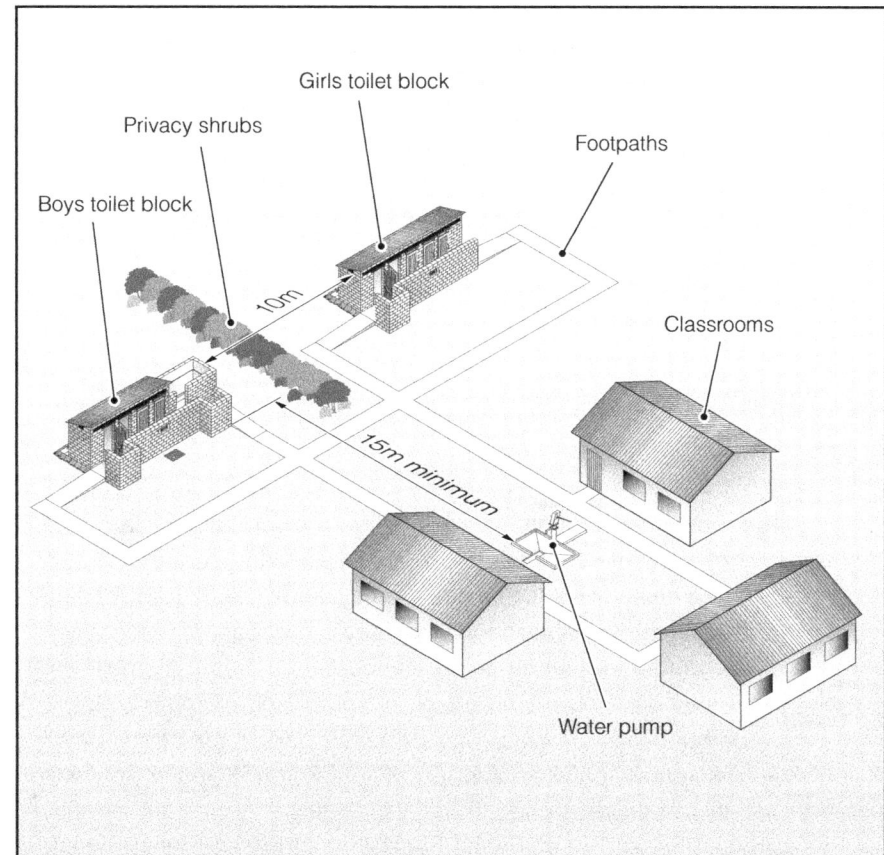

Girls toilet block

Privacy shrubs

Footpaths

Boys toilet block

10m

Classrooms

15m minimum

Water pump

Guidelines for the operation and maintenance of facilities

Day-to-day and long-term operation and maintenance

There are two aspects to the operation and maintenance of sanitation and water facilities:

- **Day-to-day** operation and maintenance – designed to keep the facilities functioning properly and in a condition that makes children and staff comfortable to use them.

- **Periodic** operation and maintenance – designed to sustain the facilities over an extended period.

Day-to-day operation and maintenance of latrines

The most important aspect of maintenance for a school latrine is to keep it clean which means, of course, making sure that regular cleaning takes place. More cleaning systems break down because of inadequate supervision than for any other reason. Generally, all that is required for cleaning is water and a brush. A small amount of disinfectant or detergent can be added to the water. Large quantities of bleach should be avoided as the strong smell will discourage children from using the latrine. Provided the floor slab is properly designed, the waste liquids should drain into the latrine. This will not affect the operation of the disposal system. If a pedestal toilet is installed, liquids should drain through the latrine wall into a soak pit.

The difficult aspect of maintaining a latrine is not *what* to do but *how* to do it. Preferences will vary. Here are the most common methods:

- **Employing cleaners.** A simple and effective way that provides additional work for members of the local community, but one which incurs a running cost.

- **Rotas.** Groups of children take turns to clean the latrines. This common method works well provided it is considered fair by the children and both boys and girls share an equal part of the process. The system has to be supervised, preferably by a teacher. The lack of interest or commitment from teachers is the most common reason for this system to fail.

- **Assigning latrines to class groups.** This approach is suitable for schools that are well provided with latrines.
A specific latrine or row of latrines is assigned to a particular group of children. Only that group use those latrines and they are responsible for cleaning them. Supervision is usually the responsibility of the class teacher or headteacher.

Whatever system of latrine cleaning is employed, it will only work safely and effectively if the cleaners are provided with protective clothing (such as boots, gloves and overalls) and cleaning equipment and materials.

The task of latrine cleaning can be made less onerous if children are taught to use the latrines properly when they first attend school. Many children start school never having used a formal toilet and therefore have no idea how to use one. Tuition in a sensitive manner early in a child's school life can save a lot of embarrassment and prevent fouled latrines later.

Some girls will begin their menstrual periods whilst still at primary school. The issue of dealing with girls' menstrual periods is extremely sensitive but a very important one when considering latrine maintenance. Soiled materials used for menstrual hygiene can be safely placed in pit latrines but alternative disposal methods must be found if any form of water borne sanitation system is used as such materials will block the pipes. A simple container with a lid in each cubicle is usually sufficient. It should be emptied regularly. The frequency will depend on the climate as well as other factors such as usage. Materials should be either incinerated or buried. If girls are expected to recycle cloths, then they need to be told to bring replacements and a bag for retaining

used materials. An additional facility for girls to wash used cloths and themselves within the girls latrine block is clearly desirable. Nonetheless the wet cloths will have to be taken home to dry.

In a society where it is customary to use absorbent material for anal cleansing it is important that appropriate materials are provided and are readily available to the children in the latrine cubicle.

It is important to maintain a regular supply of water and soap for handwashing. Many schools do not have a piped water supply and any handwashing facility will need refilling regularly. The easiest way of making sure this happens is to combine the tasks of filling the handwashing container and replenishing soap with the task of cleaning the latrine.

Periodic operation and maintenance of latrines

The latrine structure must be checked regularly and defects or breakages repaired. Children easily damage latrines through general boisterousness and ignorance. Regular maintenance will, in the long run, be cheaper than upgrading a latrine that has been left unattended.

Regular painting improves the appearance of the latrines and helps to encourage their use.

All latrines except those connected to a sewerage system will eventually need emptying. *Avoid emptying the contents of a latrine for at least six months after the latrine was last used.* Fresh excreta may contain diseases that can be harmful to the persons emptying the pit. Some harmful organisms can live for many more months. If schools have numerous latrine blocks, they can be taken out of use in succession so that only one is out of use at any one time. In most cases the contents can be dug out and buried.

The process has many potential dangers and so is best undertaken by skilled contractors.

Operating shallow pit latrines

There are some situations where it is not possible to dig a deep pit for a latrine. There may be rock close to the surface, the groundwater level may be high or the soil very soft making it difficult to dig a deep pit without the sides collapsing. In such cases a shallow pit design may be appropriate.

Shallow pits are usually about a metre deep and are divided into compartments so that each latrine cubicle can use two pits. The design works by arranging for alternate pits to be used in sequence. When one set of pits is full, the other set can be brought into use. Whilst the second set is being used, the contents of the first set can decompose during which time harmful organisms will die. When the second set of pits are full, the contents of the first set can be safely removed and the pits re-used.

The process is described in detail opposite.

How to operate a multi-compartment pit latrine

1   Use the drop hole cover provided to cover the latrine holes over pit 2 in cubicles A and B and pit 4 in cubicles C and D.

2   Cubicle A discharges waste to pit 1, cubicles B and C discharge waste to pit 3, cubicle D discharges waste to pit 5.

3   When pits 1, 3 and 5 are full (which will usually take about 2 years) move the hole covers in the cubicles so that they cover the latrine hole over pit 1 in cubicle A, pit 3 in cubicles B and C, and pit 5 in cubicle D. Cubicles A and B now discharge waste to pit 2 and cubicles C and D to pit 4.

4   When pits 2 and 4 are full (in a further 2 more years) the contents of pits 1, 3 and 5 will have become harmless and can be removed. The material removed will not smell and can safely be spread on the ground in a garden area as a soil nutrient.

5   The hole cover slabs can be moved back again to their original positions which will bring pits 1, 3 and 5 back into operation.

6   After that the contents of one set of pits will need to be emptied about every two years.

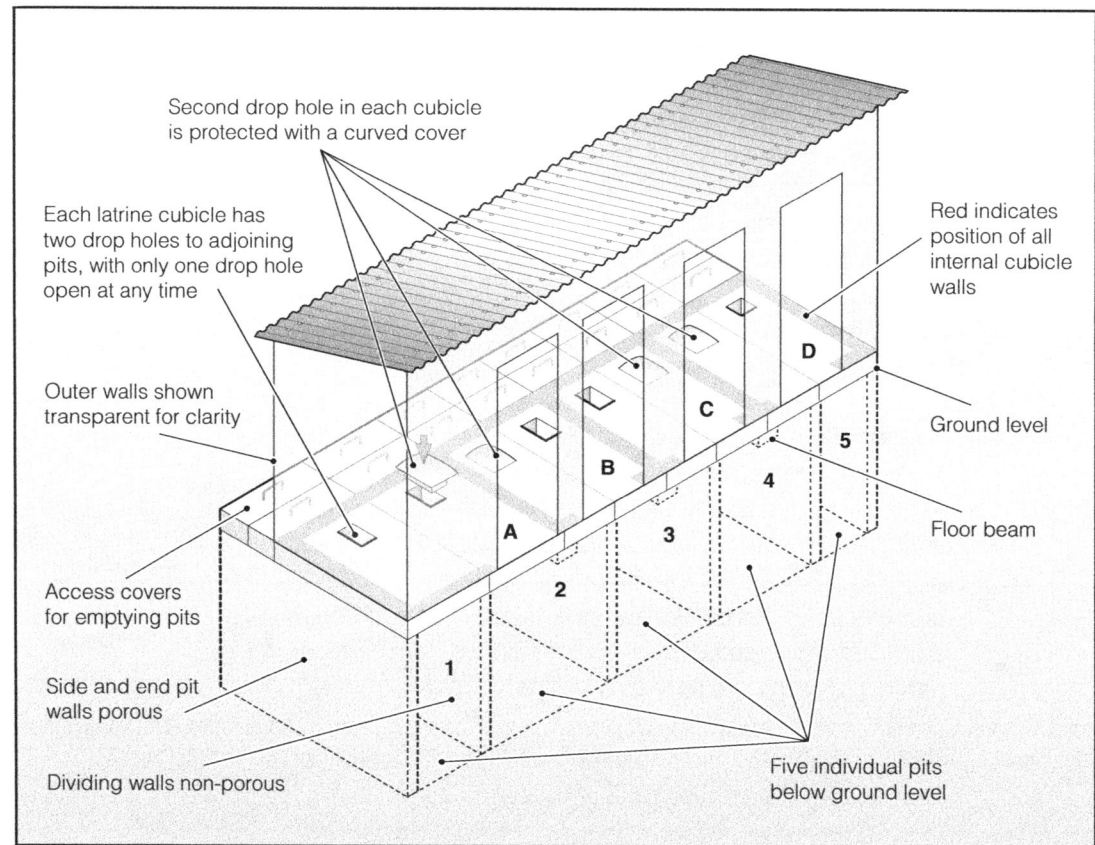

Second drop hole in each cubicle is protected with a curved cover

Each latrine cubicle has two drop holes to adjoining pits, with only one drop hole open at any time

Outer walls shown transparent for clarity

Access covers for emptying pits

Side and end pit walls porous

Dividing walls non-porous

Red indicates position of all internal cubicle walls

Ground level

Floor beam

Five individual pits below ground level

Monitoring facilities

Ideally, monitoring facilities and handwashing should take place regularly as part of school management, and not in response to impending visits from school inspectors! Realistically, however, monitoring places an additional burden on teachers so allowances may need to be made. It may be possible to involve the wider school community, such as parent-teacher associations, to carry out monitoring. Some schools form a 'sanitation committee' or appoint a 'sanitation monitor'.

There are two issues to consider with monitoring: availability and usage.

- **Availability** simply refers to the latrines being available for use. It means checking that latrines are clean and safe to use; that handwashing facilities have water and soap; that cubicle doors are fitted properly and the locks work; and that urinals are clean and the urine is being properly disposed of. Monitoring is best achieved through a participatory approach, involving children, teachers and parents to check the latrines regularly.

- **Usage** refers to monitoring the proper use of the facilities. Poor usage may be the result of vandalism or the lack of user training – or a combination of both. This type of monitoring should take place two or three times a year.

Day-to-day operation and maintenance of water points

Most water points require very little regular maintenance if they are properly designed and constructed. Common activities should include:

- checking taps and replacing washers if they are leaking (or whole units if necessary);

- cleaning the area around the water point and making sure there is no standing water;

- checking drainage channels and soak pits to make sure they are not blocked; and

- checking buckets and ropes used for drawing water from a well.

Additional maintenance is required where the only source of water is a tank filled by rainwater or tanker. These water sources frequently run dry because there is no control over their use. Children are notorious for wasting water, so tank water has to be managed. The simplest method is to allow water to be drawn at fixed times during the day only, and to assign a monitor to each tap to ensure minimal amounts of water are wasted.

Periodic operation and maintenance of water points

All water points require periodic operation and maintenance but the nature of this will depend on the type of supply and the installations. You may need to seek specific advice but the main activities are listed below.

- **Handpumps.** Check seals and valves inside the pump and bearings in the upper casing. Repair damage and cracks in the apron and drainage channel. Make sure the soakaway is operational.

- **Wells.** Repair cracks in the lining and the apron. Make sure the soakaway is operational. Remove debris from the bottom of the well.

- **Rainwater catchment.** Clean the catchment roof and guttering. Replace broken or corroded gutters. At the start of each rainy season empty the storage tank and remove silt and debris. Repair damage and cracks to the apron and drainage channel. Make sure the soakaway is operational.

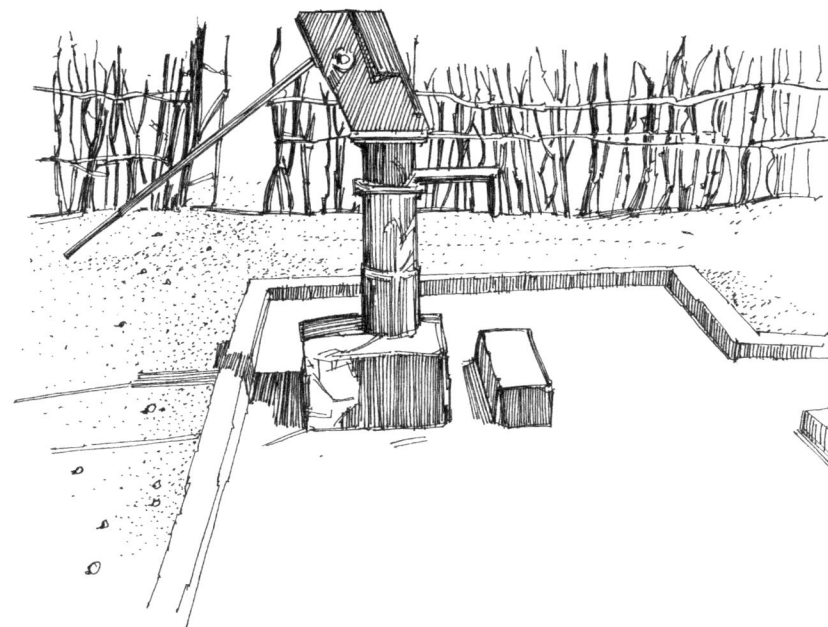

- **Springs.** Clean the area uphill from the spring. Remove dead vegetation and repair the security fence. Repair damage and cracks to the apron and drainage channel. Remove silt from storage tanks.

- **Rivers and ponds.** Repair steps and collection platforms. Remove silt from around the collection points.

- **Tap stands.** Replace worn and damaged taps. Repair damage and cracks to the apron and drainage channel. Make sure the soakaway is operational.

Guidelines for handwashing with soap

Guidelines

Why promote handwashing with soap?

Hands transport diseases from person to person either directly, or indirectly across surfaces. Hands that have been in contact with faeces, nasal excretions and other bodily fluids, and not then washed thoroughly with soap, can carry viruses, bacteria and other parasites. They also carry pathogens from contaminated sources such as animal or bird faeces, contaminated foods, or from domestic or wild animals to new susceptible hosts. Handwashing is especially important where people congregate – such as at school – where harmful organisms are more easily transmitted.

In many countries, the biggest killers of young children are respiratory infections and diarrhoeal disease. Both can be prevented by handwashing. Many reviews report a significant reduction in the risk of diarrhoea as a result of handwashing with soap. Some estimates suggest that handwashing with soap alone could prevent 0.5 – 1.4 million deaths per year.[*]

Why use soap?

Grease and dirt contain the largest concentrations of microbes. The chemical nature of soap, and the friction resulting from using it, breaks down the grease and dirt, and harmful organisms are washed away as the hands are rinsed with water.

Using soap also results in fresh and clean smelling hands, which makes the promotion of handwashing much easier. It can also help prevent eye infections.

Handwashing practice

Hands should be washed with soap and under water for at least 20 seconds. Special attention needs to be paid to germs that may be trapped under nails and in crevices.

All traces of soap should be removed with water and the hands should be dried, or allowed to dry, after cleansing and before coming into contact with anything else. The poster opposite illustrates the steps involved in washing hands thoroughly.

[*] WELL Fact Sheet: Health impact of washing hands with soap:
http://www.lboro.ac.uk/well/resources/fact-sheets/fact-sheets-htm/handwashing.htm

How to wash hands thoroughly

Hands should be washed with soap and under water for at least 20 seconds. Special attention needs to be paid to germs that may be trapped under nails and in crevices. The red arrows in the pictures below show the direction of movement of the hands.

WEDC

1. Wet hands with water

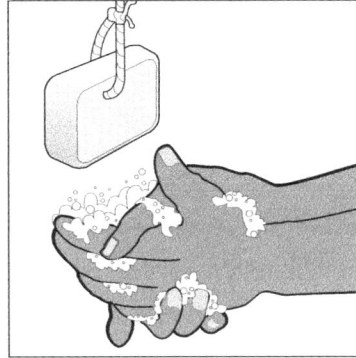

2. Apply soap to cover all surfaces of the hands

3. Rub hands palm to palm

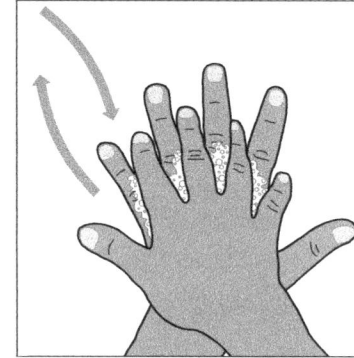

4. Rub each palm over the back of the other hand

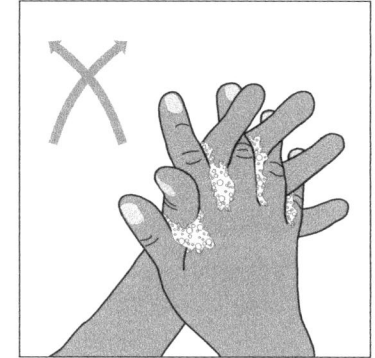

5. Rub palm to palm with fingers interlaced

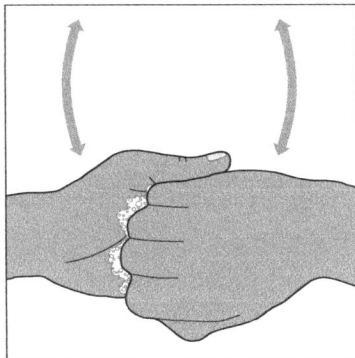

6. Rub backs of fingers to opposing palms with fingers interlocked

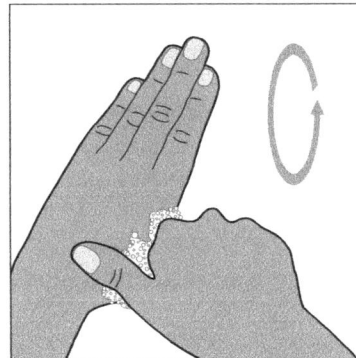

7. Rub each thumb clasped in opposing palm

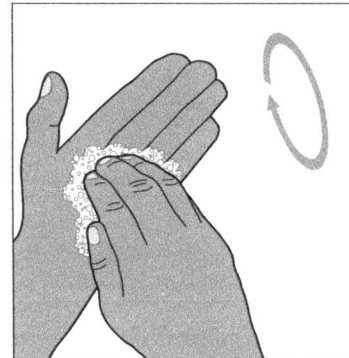

8. Clasp fingers and circular rub opposing palm

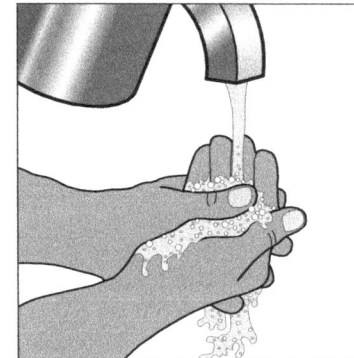

9. Rinse well with water

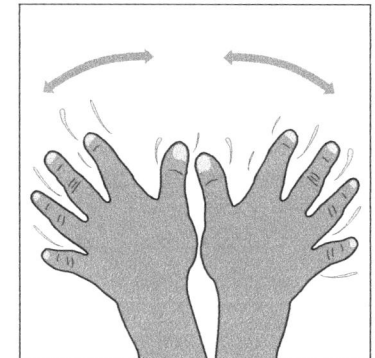

10. Allow hands to dry completely before touching anything else

Other sources of information

These related publications may also be purchased from WEDC. Order online or request a catalogue from the address given opposite.

A Guide to the Development of On-Site Sanitation

Richard Franceys, John Pickford and Bob Reed
In-depth technical information about the design, construction, operation and maintenance of the major types of on-site sanitation facility, from simple pit latrines to aqua privies and septic tanks, with numerous practical design examples.

Assessing Sanitation Policy

A series of WEDC Briefing Notes
Based on lessons learned from national sanitation policy assessments carried out in Ghana and Nepal, together with the review and assessment of sanitation policy in these and other countries. The notes provide concise guidance on the importance of sanitation policy and what can be done to ensure that it is widely supported, relevant and implemented effectively.

Drawing Water

A resource book of illustrations on water and sanitation in low-income countries   *Rod Shaw*
A book of black and white line illustrations containing over 200 images related to water supplies and sanitation in low-income countries. An invaluable resource for teachers, project managers, fieldworkers, and health professionals active in communication, education and other development work.

Guidance Manual on Water Supply and Sanitation Programmes

Designed to assist project staff and partners to develop effective and sustainable water supply and sanitation programmes. It represents collaboration across a range of professions within the Department for International Development (DFID) of the British Government and from key UK professionals. It details interdisciplinary approaches to planning and of partnership-based programmes.

Infrastructure for All

Meeting the needs of both men and women in development projects – A practical guide for engineers, technicians and project managers
Produced to help engineers, technicians and project managers ensure that the facilities they design and build are beneficial to all members of society.

Low-cost Sanitation

A survey of practical experience   *John Pickford*
A practical manual describing and comparing a range of low-cost systems – what they are, where they are appropriate, and how they can be planned, built, operated and maintained. Emphasis is given to the role of women and agencies in sanitation projects and programmes, and how householders and communities improve their own sanitation.

Low-cost Toilet Options

A catalogue   *Amaka Godfrey*

Prepared to help house owners in low-income urban communities choose an appropriate low-cost toilet option. Designed to be used by toilet builders or other NGO or government fieldworkers who support house owners in their decision. Specifically developed for use in Dar es Salaam, Tanzania, it can also be used in many other low-income communities.

Participatory Planning for Integrated Rural Water Supply and Sanitation Programmes

Guidelines and Manual   *Jeremy Ockelford and Bob Reed*

Designed to help planners and managers develop their own rural water supply and sanitation programmes.

Small-scale Water Supply

A Review of Technologies   *Brian Skinner*

Introduces the technologist and non-technologist alike to supplying water to small, low-income communities in rural areas. Details the technologies that can be used for water supply in developing countries and introduces the reader to important non-technical aspects to be considered when constructing facilities. While mainly related to point supplies such as wells, boreholes, springs and rainwater catchment systems, it also considers powered pumps, water storage, water treatment and piped distribution systems.

The Worth of Water and Running Water

Technical briefs on health, water and sanitation

Both books have 32 sections, each a reprint of a technical brief that has appeared in the journal *Waterlines* providing simple, practical guidance for fieldworkers on a variety of water and sanitation topics.

Water and Sanitation for Disabled People and Other Vulnerable Groups

Designing services to improve accessibility

Hazel Jones and Bob Reed

Based on three years of international research and collaboration with water and sanitation and disability sector organizations, this book fills a significant gap in knowledge, and will be of great interest to water and sanitation sector planners; water and sanitation service providers; organizations providing disability services; and disabled people's organizations.
(Also available in French)

**Order online at http://wedc.lboro.ac.uk/publications
or request the latest publications catalogue from WEDC.**

**WEDC Publications
The John Pickford Building
Loughborough University
Leicestershire LE11 3TU UK**
*Phone: +44 (0) 1509 222885
Email: wedc-publications@lboro.ac.uk*

Glossary

Definitions of some common terms used in this book

apron	a contained area surrounding a water-point designed to drain wastewater, usually made of concrete
backfill	material used to refill an excavated area
decommission	to withdraw from active use
excreta	waste matter, including urine and faeces, discharged from the body
faeces	waste matter discharged from the bowels; excrement
microbe	micro-organism, especially one that causes disease
non-porous	not able to be permeated by fluids
organism	a living being, an individual animal or plant
pathogen	an agent that causes disease, especially a living micro-organism such as a bacterium or fungus
peri-urban area	an outlying inhabited area of a large city
porous	containing pores, able to be permeated by fluids

pour-flush	a method of discharging excreta into a latrine using water
rehabilitate	to restore to good condition, operation, or capacity
shallow pit	a pit up to 1.5 metres deep
soakaway / soak pit	a pit used to absorb waste fluids into the ground
superstructure	the latrine shelter; the visible component of the latrine above ground-level
virus	a sub-microscopic particle that can infect the cells of a biological organism but cannot replicate themselves without infecting a host cell

About WEDC

WEDC is one of the world's leading education and research institutes for improving access to infrastructure and services for the poor in low- and middle-income countries. We are based in the Department of Civil and Building Engineering at Loughborough University in the UK, but we work all over the world.

Education and training with WEDC

WEDC offers a variety of education and training programmes at postgraduate level including MSc and Diploma programmes. They are modular, so programmes may be studied to suit individual needs – based on core modules and a choice from a range of optional modules. A number of the modules can be studied by distance learning as an alternative to studying at Loughborough. Programmes include:

- Water and Waste Engineering
- Water and Environmental Management
- Sustainable Infrastructure Services Management
- Sustainability in the Built Environment
- Infrastructure in Emergencies

Research and consultancy

WEDC research is directed towards the study of all aspects of infrastructure and services for development in low- and middle-income countries.

Our work ranges from studies of specific technical problems to broadly based investigations involving the integration of management, technology, finance, economic, and sociological components.

We focus on the problems faced by policymakers, professionals, practitioners and communities in developing countries, and investigate feasible solutions. Dissemination includes publication of guidelines on best practice and case studies from cities, towns and villages worldwide.

The WEDC International Conference, which is held alternately in Asia and Africa, provides a forum for exchange of research and experience on improving infrastructure and services for development.

Our consultancy work is also primarily concerned with low- and middle-income countries.